WORKBOOK
with Digital Pack

5

CEFR
C1

TH!NK

SECOND EDITION

T0384508

Herbert Puchta,
Jeff Stranks &
Peter Lewis-Jones
with Clare Kennedy

ACKNOWLEDGEMENTS

Acknowledgements

The authors and publishers acknowledge the following sources of copyright material and are grateful for the permissions granted. While every effort has been made, it has not always been possible to identify the sources of all the material used, or to trace all copyright holders. If any omissions are brought to our notice, we will be happy to include the appropriate acknowledgements on reprinting and in the next update to the digital edition, as applicable.

Keys: UW = Unit Welcome; U = Unit.

Text

U5: Financial Times for the text adapted from 'On your bike, son – family bonding on a motorbike', by Simon de Burton, *Financial Times*, 30.11.2020. Copyright © 2020 The Financial Times Ltd.

Photography

The following photographs are sourced from Getty Images.

UW: william87/iStock/Getty Images Plus; **U1**: Stockbyte; Dustin Finkelstein/ Getty Images Entertainment; Alina555/E+; fizkes/iStock/Getty Images Plus; Daisy-Daisy/iStock/Getty Images Plus; Vladimir Godnik; Uwe Krejci/DigitalVision; Daniela Duncan/Moment Open; Barry Austin/Photodisc; **U2**: Alex Wong/Getty Images News; Steve Granitz/WireImage; Chip Somodevilla/Getty Images News; Eamonn McCormack/WireImage; Flashpop/Stone; **U3**: Neustockimages/E+; SensorSpot/E+; Carlina Teteris/Moment; hopsalka/iStock/Getty Images Plus; Eva Katalin Kondoros/iStock/Getty Images Plus; Dmitry Belyaev/iStock/Getty Images Plus; ArtMarie/E+; **U4**: fstop123/E+; CBS Photo Archive; John Rowley; Maica/E+; **U5**: Education Images/Universal Images Group; FREDDUFOUR/Staff/ AFP; Chicago Tribune/Tribune News Service; Daniel Berehulak/Getty Images News; dennisvdw/iStock/Getty Images Plus; **U6**: Taylor Hill/FilmMagic; scanrail/ iStock/Getty Images Plus; JORGE GUERRERO/AFP; Robert Alexander/Archive Photos; **U7**: RyanJLane/E+; guenterguni/iStock/Getty Images Plus; Jason_V/E+; Jay Paull/Archive Photos; GeorgiosArt/iStock/Getty Images Plus; **U8**: REDA&CO/ Universal Images Group; Scar1984/iStock/Getty Images Plus; Joe Sohm/Visions of America/Universal Images Group; zoranm/E+; **U9**: kaanates/iStock/Getty Images Plus; Digital Vision/Photodisc; monkeybusinessimages/iStock/Getty Images Plus; **U10**: SilviaJansen/iStock/Getty Images Plus; furtaev/iStock/Getty Images Plus; Aaron McCoy/The Image Bank; **U11**: Ghislain & Marie David de Lossy/The Image Bank; beppeverge/Moment; Martin Wahlborg/iStock/Getty Images Plus; **U12**: Thomas Janisch/Moment; simonkr/E+; TONY KARUMBA/AFP; Yiming Chen/Moment; DC_Colombia/iStock/Getty Images Plus.

The following photographs are sourced from other libraries.

U4: Iakov Filimonov/Shutterstock; **U9** & **U12**: Pictorial Press Ltd/Alamy Stock Photo; **U10**: VectorMine/Alamy Stock Vector.

Cover photography by Cover photography by jonya/E+/Getty Images; muratart/ Shutterstock.

Illustrations

UW, U2, U4, U9, U11: David Semple; **UW, U1, U2, U3, U6**: Julian Mosedale; **U4**: Bryan Beach (Advocate Art); **U6, U7**: Carl Harrison; **U8**: Tracey Knight (Lemonade).

Video stills

Grammar Video Stills production by Silversun Media Group.

Audio Production by Sonica Studios Limited.

CONTENTS

WELCOME

A LESSONS IN LIFE
Saying *yes* and adding conditions

1 **Match the sentence halves.**

1 I'll take you to the party as long ☐
2 We'll buy you a laptop provided ☐
3 I won't let you use my tablet unless ☐
4 Stop arguing about the TV. Otherwise ☐

a you agree to our rules about using it.
b I'll turn it off.
c as you give me a hand in the garden.
d you help me with my homework first.

2 **Rewrite the sentences using the word in brackets.**

1 If you don't promise to not tell anyone,
   I won't tell you my secret. (unless)

   _____

2 You can borrow my phone, but you mustn't
   use all the data. (provided)

   _____

3 If you promise to be back before midnight,
   you can go to the party. (long)

   _____

4 If we don't keep the noise down, my
   neighbour is going to get very angry.
   (otherwise)

   _____

get used to

1 **Put the words in order to make sentences.**

1 get / this / never / I'll / messaging / used / on /
   phone / to

   _____

2 new / few / took / used / to / school / me /
   months / to / It / get / a / my

   _____

3 used / might / new / while / It / using / you /
   the / take / get / to / a / system / to

   _____

4 Saturdays / got / early / on / finally / getting /
   used / up / to / I've

   _____

2 <audio> W.02 **Listen and write what the speaker says under the correct picture.**

A _____   C _____

B _____   D _____

Friendship idioms

1 **Circle the correct word in each friendship idiom.**

1 fall *out / over*
2 know someone inside *over / out*
3 look like two peas *in / with* a pod
4 get on like a house *into / on* fire
5 have a shoulder to cry *on / over*
6 bury *a / the* hatchet
7 be joined *at / around* the hip
8 clear *for / the* air

2 **Complete the missing words with friendship idioms from Exercise 1.**

1 I really don't agree with Sam, but for the sake of our
   friendship, I've decided to _____ .
2 The atmosphere was so unpleasant that she decided it was
   time to _____ .
3 People say we rushed into getting married, but I don't
   agree – Sally and I _____ .
4 Let's not talk about this right now. I really don't want to
   _____ about this.
5 My best friend Tom and I could be brothers. Our mums say
   we are like _____ .
6 When Rory met my parents, they got on like
   _____ . I was so relieved!
7 Isabella needed a _____ after she lost
   her job, so she came over to see me yesterday evening.
8 Those two are always together. They seem to be
   _____ .

SUMMING UP

1 Put the dialogue in order.

☐ **Freya** I said I wanted to settle down with Jack one day and start a family.

☐ **Freya** Not really. She asked everyone.

☐ **Freya** Well money isn't everything. I could get used to having less money but I couldn't live without happiness.

1 **Freya** Miss Jones asked me today what I wanted to do with my life.

☐ **Freya** Well of course I do, but only as long as I don't fall out with Jack over it.

☐ **Tom** That's a strange question for a teacher to ask.

☐ **Tom** Well I hope you get what you want.

☐ **Tom** So what did you tell her?

☐ **Tom** But don't you want a career too?

☐ **Tom** That's quite an old-fashioned idea. Most people these days are more worried about making money.

B CHALLENGES
Verbs with *-ing* or infinitive

1 Complete the sentences with the correct form of the verbs.

1 meet

  a Nico's mad at me because I forgot _____ him at the station.

  b I'll never forget _____ my husband for the first time.

2 call

  a I tried _____ you, but my phone was dead.

  b Have you tried _____ her mobile? She never answers her landline number.

3 say

  a I really regret _____ those things. It was really mean.

  b We regret _____ that we cannot accept your entry for the competition because the deadline was yesterday.

4 take

  a Please remember _____ back the library books. They're due back today.

  b I don't remember _____ that photo, but I do remember that day.

5 chat

  a Miss Green told me to stop _____ five times today.

  b I met Anya on my way home and we stopped _____ for an hour.

2 Complete the sentences with your own ideas.

1 I really regret _____ . I feel terrible about it.

2 Today I really mustn't forget _____ .

3 I must stop _____ . It's such a bad habit.

4 I don't remember _____ when I was younger.

5 If you're finding it difficult to get to sleep, try _____ .

Issuing and accepting a challenge

1 Complete the words then match the sentences. There are two replies you do not need.

1 I b ___ ___ you can't eat all that pizza. ☐

2 I c ___ ___ l ___ ___ n ___ ___ ___ you to a race to the bus stop. ☐

3 Do you r ___ c ___ ___ ___ you could last a day without using your phone? ☐

4 I ___ e ___ I can finish before you. ☐

a You're probably right, but I don't really care. I'm in no hurry.

b OK, you're on. Last there pays for the ticket.

c That's too easy. I'm really good at swimming.

d Of course I could, but why would I want to?

e I bet I can. I'm starving.

f You'll never manage to last a whole day.

2 Complete the dialogues with your own ideas.

1 **A** Do you reckon you could _____ _____ ?

  B That's too easy. I've got a really good memory.

2 **A** I challenge you to _____ _____ .

  B Not now. I'm much too tired.

3 **A** I bet I can _____ _____ .

  B No way. You'll never manage to do it.

4 **A** I bet you can't _____ _____ .

  B You're right. Tell me.

Our greatest challenge

1 **Complete the sentences with the words in the list.**

> apprehensive | believe | feeling
> positive | unsure | worried

1 I'm really _____ about my date with Izzy.
2 I'm a bit _____ about whether I should play in the football match after school.
3 I'm feeling quite _____ about the English exam tomorrow.

4 I feel quite _____ about my life.
5 I've got a really good _____ about the next few years.
6 I _____ things will work out for the best.

2 **Add a reason for each of the sentences in Exercise 1.**

1 *I haven't got anything to wear.* _____
2 _____
3 _____
4 _____
5 _____
6 _____

Phrases for talking about the future

1 **Complete the sentences with the words in the list.**

> about to | certain | likely to | off to | on the point of

1 They are _____ the moon.

4 We are _____ lose this match, I think.

2 He is _____ lose his temper.

5 They are _____ to miss the bus.

3 She's _____ reaching the top.

SUMMING UP

1 **🔊 W.03 Complete the dialogue with the words in the list. There are four extra words. Then listen and check.**

> about | apprehensive | bet | certain
> challenge | doing | feeling | off
> positive | right | to do | to feel

Lucy I ¹_____ you to come with me on the new ride.

Eric What! You know how ²_____ those things make me.

Lucy Come on. You've been on one before.

Eric I know and I remember ³_____ terrified the whole time.

Lucy Well, I'll be with you this time. I ⁴_____ I can help you forget your fear.

Eric You're probably ⁵_____, but maybe later.

Lucy We haven't got any time. The ride's ⁶_____ to close.

Eric We'll just have to come back another day, then.

Lucy You'll regret not ⁷_____ it if we leave now.

Eric Maybe I will, but I'm ⁸_____ to get an ice-cream before the café closes. I'd regret that even more.

C EMPATHISING

Cheering someone up and sympathising about past situations

1 Complete the 'sympathising' expressions.

1 Don't let _____ .
2 What a _____ .
3 Poor _____ .
4 Cheer _____ .
5 How _____ .
6 Hang _____ .
7 Oh, _____ .
8 Look on _____ .

2 Complete the dialogues with your own ideas.

1 A _____
  B Oh dear. I hope he'll buy you another one.
2 A _____
  B What a shame. And you worked so hard for it.
3 A _____
  B How terrible. I know how much you were looking forward to it.
4 A _____
  B Hang in there. I'm sure he'll get better soon.
5 A _____
  B Don't let it get you down. There are hundreds of other things you can do.
6 A _____
  B Look on the bright side. At least you saved yourself a lot of money.

Life's ups and downs

1 Complete the sentences with the phrases in the list.

> blame | didn't live up to my expectations
> getting in the way of | let her down
> my way | tried my hardest

1 That film was terrible – it certainly _____ .
2 I _____ to apologise but she just wouldn't listen to me.
3 There's no one to _____ but yourself.
4 I can't believe you forgot – she was really looking forward to going out with you – you really _____ .
5 Nothing's going _____ today – I should have stayed in bed.
6 My phone hasn't stopped ringing – all these calls are really _____ my homework.

2 Complete the dialogues with the sentences from Exercise 1.

1 **Dan** What's up with you? You've burnt your toast and spilled your coffee!
  Gabi ☐
2 **Pete** Mum, I haven't done my homework. The teacher's going to kill me.
  Mum ☐
3 **Claudia** Well, that was a massive disappointment!
  Tim Really? I thought it was good.
  Claudia ☐
4 **Lucy** Hi, Mum. I'm home.
  Mum But you were supposed to go to your grandmother's.
  Lucy What? Oh no, it's Thursday. I forgot!
  Mum ☐
5 **Toni** You've spent all morning on the computer, Grace.
  Grace ☐
6 **Clara** Amanda's really upset with you.
  Josh I know. ☐

Adjectives to describe uncomfortable feelings

1 Add the missing vowels to make words to describe uncomfortable feelings.

1 stck _____
2 glty _____
3 shmd _____
4 wkwrd _____
5 pzzld _____
6 dsprt _____

2 Use the words from Exercise 1 to describe how these people feel.

1 'I don't know why I said that to him. It was a terrible thing to do.' _____
2 'Why would she behave like that? It's not like her at all.' _____
3 'I know I shouldn't have but I read your text.' _____
4 'It's no good. I really can't see the answer to this Maths problem.' _____
5 'Please help me. Please. I really don't know what to do. I'll do anything … ' _____
6 'She's your sister – not your girlfriend? Oh dear. Sorry about that.' _____

Talking about past ability

1 **Match the sentence halves.**

1 She managed to get the car started and ☐
2 We succeeded in completing the game and ☐
3 She managed to stop the baby crying and ☐
4 He didn't succeed in persuading the police officer and ☐
5 I didn't manage to fix the TV and ☐
6 We didn't succeed in finding a hotel and ☐

a we were able to get to sleep.
b he wasn't able to continue his journey.
c we weren't able to watch the match.
d she was able to continue her journey.
e we weren't able to spend the night there.
f we were able to get to the next level.

2 **Compete the sentences with your own ideas about last weekend.**

1 I was able to _____ .
2 I succeeded in _____ .
3 I managed to _____ .
4 I wasn't able to _____ .
5 I didn't succeed in _____ .
6 I didn't manage to _____ .

SUMMING UP

1 **Complete the dialogue with the missing words. There are four extra words.**

> ashamed | blame | bright | dear | fault
> let | light | made | managed | puzzled
> succeeded | you

Tim Hey Jen, how did the match go? Tell me you
¹_____ to score a goal.

Jen I don't really want to talk about it.

Tim Oh ²_____ . What happened?

Jen The only thing I ³_____ in doing was to make a complete fool of myself.

Tim It can't have been that bad.

Jen Well it was. I ⁴_____ the whole team down.

Tim How? What went so wrong?

Jen The game finished 1–1, so there was a penalty shoot-out. I missed the penalty and we lost.

Tim Poor ⁵_____ .

Jen I'm so ⁶_____ . It's all my fault.

Tim Don't be silly. It could have happened to anyone. You can't ⁷_____ yourself.

Jen Well I do. I'll never be chosen to play again.

Tim I'm sure you will, but even if you don't, look on the ⁸_____ side. You can hang out with me more.

D BUT IS IT NEWS?
Introducing news

1 **Match the statements (1–5) with the responses (a–e).**

1 Have you heard? ☐
2 Have you heard about Sylvie? ☐
3 Did you know Mr Thomas has had an accident? ☐
4 Guess what. ☐
5 You'll never believe what I heard! ☐

a No, what happened?
b So tell me. What did you hear?
c Heard what?
d What?
e No, what's she done now?

2 **Write a third line for each dialogue in Exercise 1.**

1 _____
2 _____
3 _____
4 _____
5 _____

Ways of speaking

1 **What are these people doing? Match the sentences with the verbs in the list.**

> announcing | complaining | confessing
> introducing | recommending

1 If you like spicy food, you should try this recipe.
_____

2 Ok, it was me who took the money but I was going to put it back, I promise. _____

3 Why is there never anything good on TV on a Friday night? _____

4 Olivia, I'd like you to meet Tom.
_____

5 I'd just like to say that Mr Palmer will be leaving the school in April after teaching here for 15 years.
_____

verb + noun collocations with *make, take, play, do, give*

1 Write the nouns in the list under the correct verb headings. Sometimes there is more than one possible answer.

> a deal | a decision | a part | a speech
> advantage | advice | money | progress
> research | revenge

make

_____
_____
_____
_____
_____

play

_____
_____
_____
_____

give

_____
_____
_____
_____

take

_____
_____
_____
_____

do

_____
_____
_____
_____

2 Complete the sentences with collocations from Exercise 1.

1 They want an answer tomorrow, so we need to _____ soon.
2 The UN _____ an important _____ in ending the conflict.
3 _____ my _____ and don't say anything to him.
4 Scientists are _____ into a cure for the disease.
5 I had to _____ in front of the whole school. I was terrified.
6 They _____ a lot of _____ buying old houses and restoring them. It's a very profitable business.

Cause and effect linkers

1 Complete the sentences with words in the list.

> because | consequently | due | result

1 As a _____ of our excellent exam results, our teacher has said we can have an end-of-term party.
2 Not many people knew about the party. _____ , not many people turned up.
3 All the trains were cancelled _____ of very bad weather.
4 We were late _____ to a massive traffic jam on the motorway.

2 Complete the sentences with your own ideas.

1 I had a really bad headache this morning. Consequently, _____ .
2 I couldn't get to sleep last night because of _____ .
3 As a result of doing really well in my exams _____ .
4 I'm not able to come to your party due to _____ .

Sharing news

1 Circle the correct words.

1 If you see Dan, can you *let / make / allow* him know that the party has been cancelled?
2 I know you'll only be away for a year, but you must promise to *get / keep / continue* in touch.
3 I need to *keep / get / make* in touch with Suzi. Can you text me her number?
4 I've got a place on the course. I can't wait to *make / take / break* the news to my parents.
5 Ms Sperry asked me to *give / pass / push* on a message that she's going to be five minutes late.

SUMMING UP

1 Put the conversation in the correct order.

☐	**Dad**	That's your problem, not mine.
☐	**Dad**	No, Sophie. I'm sorry. There are no more chances. From now on, you're on your own in the kitchen.
☐	**Dad**	Guess what, kids. I have made a decision.
1	**Dad**	Everyone, I'd like to announce something.
☐	**Dad**	I will. Because of the mess that you always leave in the kitchen, I am no longer going to make meals for you.
☐	**Will**	I don't really think it's a problem. I quite like the idea of cooking for myself.
☐	**Will**	What is it this time, Dad?
☐	**Sophie**	That's not fair, Dad. How are we supposed to eat?
☐	**Sophie**	That's because you don't really care what you eat. But I do. Please Dad. Give us another chance.
☐	**Sophie**	Come on then. Tell us what it is.

1 FAMILY MATTERS

Grammar video

▶ 02

Ⓖ GRAMMAR
Talking about habits

⟶ SB p.14

1 ★☆☆ **Tick (✓) the sentences that refer to habits.**

1 My parents didn't use to take us on holiday. ☐
2 I'm meeting Sara for a coffee later. ☐
3 My sister will talk for hours if you let her. ☐
4 I used to watch TV every day after school. ☐
5 Charlie tends to leave his homework until the last minute. ☐
6 I can't believe my dad will be 50 next week. ☐
7 My aunt Abi would always get me the most amazing presents for my birthday. ☐
8 My little brothers are always asking me questions. ☐

2 ★★☆ **Look at the sentences in Exercise 1 again. Do they refer to past, present or future?**

3 ★★☆ **Complete the text with the words or phrases in the list.**

> always make | are always trying
> tends to be | used to | used to keep
> will always | would | would never

I ¹_____ be quite shy when I was younger. There was always a lot of noise at home and I ²_____ just sit quietly in the corner reading a book. It was the same at school. I ³_____ put my hand up when the teacher asked a question. I ⁴_____ quiet and hope she wouldn't pick me.
I'm certainly not shy any more. I can't be. I'm a magician and I provide entertainment at children's parties. It's a lot of fun but it ⁵_____ a little chaotic. The children ⁶_____ to find out how I do my tricks. At the end of my show I ⁷_____ an elephant out of balloons. Of course, all the kids want it, but I ⁸_____ give it to the one child who's sat quietly without making too much of a fuss. After all, I know exactly how they feel.

4 ★★☆ **Complete the second sentence so that it has a similar meaning to the first sentence using the word given. Do not change the word. Use between three and six words, including the word given.**

0 I was quite jealous of my younger brother when I was little.
   USED
   I _____used to be_____ quite jealous of my younger brother when I was little.

1 My sister takes my things without asking and it's really annoying.
   ALWAYS
   My sister is _____ without asking.

2 My grandma has a habit of getting our names mixed up.
   TENDS
   My grandma _____ mixed up.

3 Younger children tend to stay in the family home for longer.
   WILL
   Younger children _____ their parents for longer.

4 I never really got on with my brother when I lived at home.
   USE
   I _____ with my brother when I lived at home.

5 My sister and I used to sometimes have fights.
   WOULD
   My sister and I _____ fights.

5 ★★★ **Complete the sentences so that they are true for you.**

1 I didn't use to _____ when I was little.

2 I tend to _____ when I'm tired.

3 In the school holidays my family would _____ .

4 I will sometimes _____ when I'm hungry.

5 My best friend is always _____ .

10

Adverbs to express attitude → SB p.17

6 ⭐☆☆ **Complete the mini-dialogues with the adverbs in the list.**

> admittedly | annoyingly
> honestly | hopefully | surely

1 A _____ , my parents have decided we're not going to Majorca this year.
  B That's a shame. I know you were really looking forward to practising your Spanish.

2 A Are you going to miss your brother when he goes to university next week?
  B _____ , I don't think I will and I can't wait to have a bedroom all to myself.

3 A _____ you must be proud of your sister winning the singing competition?
  B I suppose I am. The problem is that she won't stop talking about it.

4 A You can't be very happy your brother's taken up the trumpet.
  B Well, _____ , he'll lose interest in it after a few days.

5 A I can't believe you said that to Lucy.
  B _____ , it was a bit mean, but sometimes she just really annoys me.

7 ⭐☆☆ **Choose the correct options.**

Fri 1st May

¹*Honestly / Surely / Regrettably*, I'm going to win the school art competition, aren't I? I mean my picture's the best by far. ²*Hopefully / Admittedly / Understandably*, the judges will see that and give me first place. ³*Surely / Obviously / Admittedly*, Tanya Baker's painting is quite good, but not as good as mine.

Mon 4th May

⁴*Hopefully / Honestly / Regrettably*, I didn't get first place in the art competition. I can't quite believe it. ⁵*Honestly / Regrettably / Admittedly*, I really thought that prize was mine. ⁶*Annoyingly / Understandably / Surely*, I'm upset at the moment. ⁷*Understandably / Annoyingly / Admittedly*, the judges decided that Tanya Baker's watercolour painting of a boat was better than my abstract impression of a puddle. ⁸*Surely / Hopefully / Obviously*, they don't know anything about art.

8 ⭐⭐☆ **Rewrite the sentences using the adverb form of the underlined words.**

0 The bus was late, which was <u>annoying</u>.
  Annoyingly, the bus was late.

1 I <u>hope</u> I'll get chosen for the school play.
  _____

2 It's <u>obvious</u> that he wasn't happy about what you said.
  _____

3 If I'm <u>honest</u> I don't really care what you do.
  _____

4 They sold all their best players, which was <u>regrettable</u>.
  _____

5 I have to <u>admit</u> that I didn't really try very hard.
  _____

6 It's <u>understandable</u> that they were quite upset about their test results.
  _____

7 I'm <u>sure</u> it won't rain again today.
  _____

GET IT *RIGHT!*

Adverbs to express attitude

Learners often put adverbs in the wrong position in the sentence.

✓ *Regrettably, I can't come to your party.*
✗ *I ~~regrettably~~ can't come to your party.*

Put the words in order to make sentences. Add commas where necessary.

1 get on / my brother and I / hopefully / start / to / better / now / might
  _____

2 new job / regrettably / my / things / just / made / worse
  _____

3 her / doesn't / if / Nora / start / more / respectful / to / teachers / she'll / into / get / honestly / trouble / being
  _____

4 agree / admittedly / don't / on / we / but / still / are / everything / good / we / friends
  _____

5 upset / very / about / you're / behaviour / understandably / inconsiderate / his
  _____

6 were / obviously / used / a / teacher / lazy students / the / not / to / such / having / demanding
  _____

VOCABULARY
Personality (1)

→ SB p.14

1 ★☆☆ **Match the adjectives with the pictures.**

> insecure | rebellious | respectful
> self-centred | traditional | unconventional

1 _____

4 _____

2 _____

5 _____

3 _____

6 _____

2 ★★☆ **Match the sentences.**

1 My cousin's really outgoing. ☐
2 Don't be so insecure. ☐
3 Laura's very self-centred. ☐
4 I was pretty rebellious as a child. ☐
5 Some of his ideas are quite unconventional. ☐
6 Your friend Adriana's not very respectful. ☐
7 My parents are very traditional. ☐
8 My dad's really demanding. ☐

a In fact, the way she treats her parents is quite rude.
b I used to do the exact opposite of what my parents said.
c He wants me home by 10 pm every night!
d She rarely thinks about anyone but herself.
e They don't always understand different points of view.
f You're a wonderful person. You really are.
g We don't always agree, but he's interesting to talk to.
h He loves meeting new people.

3 ★★★ **Write a short paragraph about yourself. Choose four of the adjectives in Exercise 2 and say why they apply (or don't apply) to you.**

_____
_____
_____
_____
_____
_____
_____

Personal conflict

→ SB p.17

4 ★★☆ **Complete the text with the words in the list.**

> fights | life | me | nerves | put
> something | things | word

He's been ¹*making my* _____ *miserable* for six months now. At first it wasn't too bad. He was exciting and new, but he soon started to ²*get on my* _____ . It was just little things at first, like the noises he would make and always being wherever I was. And now every morning, as soon as I wake up, before I'm even out of bed – 'How are you today?' Why can't he just ³*let* _____ *be*?

I'm also not the sort of person who usually ⁴*gets into* _____ with other people and there's certainly no point with him. I'd ⁵*have a* _____ *with* him about his behaviour but, of course, I can't. And there's no danger of me ⁶*saying* _____ *I might regret* – he doesn't understand a word I say.

To ⁷*make* _____ *worse*, he thinks I actually like him. Or does he? I'm beginning to wonder if he's trying to take over my life. I'm not sure how much longer I can ⁸_____ *up with* him.

'Your new best friend for life,' that's what it said on the box. Well, he isn't and I'm beginning to regret the day I decided to buy myself the RoboFriend 200X.

5 ★★☆ **Match the expressions in italics in Exercise 4 with the definitions a–h.**

a being really unkind to someone over a long period of time ☐
b have a serious talk with someone about something you're not happy about ☐
c increase a bad situation ☐
d really annoy someone ☐
e willing to accept someone or something that is not pleasant or desirable ☐
f express something bad out of anger or frustration ☐
g leave someone alone and not bother them ☐
h to have or cause arguments with other people ☐

REFERENCE

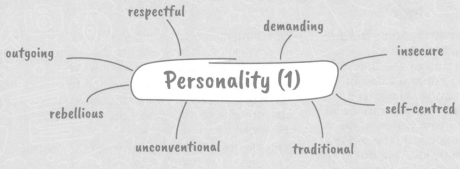

respectful

demanding

outgoing

insecure

Personality (1)

self-centred

rebellious

unconventional traditional

get on (my) nerves

get into fights with

say something (you)
might regret

let (somebody) be

Personal conflict

make things worse
(for somebody)

have a word with
(somebody)

put up with somebody/
something

make (somebody's)
life miserable

VOCABULARY EXTRA

1   **Match the expressions with the definitions.**

1	set up home	a	to give people in a family the things they need, for example food, clothes, money
2	bring up children	b	a quality or ability that many members of the same family have
3	provide for a family	c	care for children until they are adults
4	run in the family	d	feel like you belong or are part of a family
5	be like one of the family	e	to have everything you need to create a home in new accommodation or a new place

2   **Complete the sentences with the correct expressions from Exercise 1.**

1   Eric isn't my brother. He's my friend, but he's just _____ .

2   My parents moved here when they got married and they _____ together.

3   Blue eyes _____ , but mine are brown.

4   It isn't always easy to _____ , but it's usually a very rewarding experience.

5   It's important to _____ material things
_____ , but emotional support is also very important.

3   **Answer the questions about you.**

1   What qualities or physical features run in your family?

_____

2   Where do you want to set up home? Why?

_____

3   What do you think are the most important things to provide for a family? Why?

_____

Long-lost ...

One day in December 2012, Anaïs Bordier (a French student studying fashion in London) was surprised to see that another student had posted a video of her on her Facebook page. Anaïs was intrigued because she had never made a video of herself. When she watched the video, the mystery deepened. The girl in the video looked exactly like her, but it was not her. Unfortunately, as there was no name on the video, there was no way of investigating any further.

About a month later, Anaïs came across another video of the same girl. It was a trailer for a film. Suddenly, she had a lead. She investigated and found from the cast list that the girl's name was Samantha Futerman. She was an actress in the US. She also found out that they shared the same birthday. But even more surprising, Samantha, like herself, had been born in South Korea.

Anaïs had always known that she was adopted. She knew she had been born in the city of Busan in South Korea, the only child of a young, unmarried woman. She had been adopted by a French couple and had spent her life in France. But now she was starting to question whether or not she knew the whole truth. She phoned her mother who asked the question she had secretly been asking herself: could she have a twin?

Anaïs decided to get in touch with Samantha and send her a message. She told Samantha to check out her Facebook page.

When Samantha got back in touch, she sent a copy of her adoption certificate. They had been born in the same hospital. It was official. They were twins!

They exchanged photos and arranged to speak online. Anaïs was amazed. They had the same laugh, the same facial movements. They even had similar haircuts. They spoke for three hours.

Eventually the girls decided to meet. Samantha, accompanied by her parents and brothers, flew over to London. Anaïs took her mother and a few friends along to the meeting for moral support. But there was no need. As soon as they came face-to-face, the girls knew they wanted to be alone and catch up on all the missing years. So they went off to have lunch, stopping every couple of minutes to check out their reflections in shop windows to make sure it wasn't all just a dream. Later that day, the girls received more news. They weren't just twins, they were also identical twins.

Anaïs still wonders why they were separated at birth. Samantha said that she had once tried to make contact with their birth mother, but the woman named on the adoption papers had told her she had the wrong person. But for Anaïs, none of this matters now. She has found a sister who she didn't even know existed, and although they live on different continents, they spend as much time as they possibly can together.

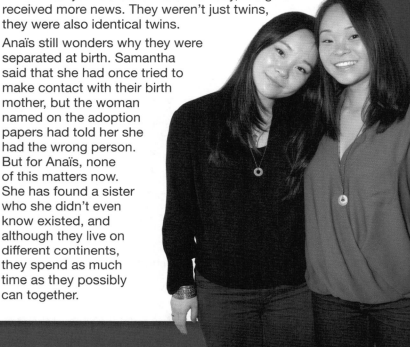

📖 READING

1 Read the true story. How are Anaïs and Samantha related?

2 Read the story again and put the events in the order they happened.

- [ ] Anaïs finds out information about the mystery girl.
- [ ] Anaïs and her mother wonder if she could have a twin.
- [ ] The girls get together.
- [ ] Anaïs makes contact with Samantha.
- [ ] Anaïs watches a video of someone who looks just like her.
- [ ] Anaïs gets confirmation she's a twin.
- [ ] Anaïs learns that she is adopted.
- [ ] The girls find out exactly how they are related.

3 Imagine Samantha and Anaïs' first online call and write a short dialogue (8–10 lines).

4 **CRITICAL THINKING** Read the opinions. Which ones are for (F) or against (A) using social media to contact people? Add some opinions of your own.

1 If I had wanted to keep in touch with people, I would have done it anyway. [ ]

2 It's such a great way to find friends and relatives you thought you'd lost contact with. [ ]

3 You don't need social media to contact people. It's like spying on them. [ ]

4 For me, it's been an amazing way to discover more about my family's history and build my family tree. [ ]

DEVELOPING { *Writing*

Writing a personal email

1 INPUT **Read Lola's email and answer the questions.**

1 What is Lola's big news?
_____

2 Who is Jennie?
_____

3 Why does Lola admire her so much?
_____

To: saskia99@mymail.com
Subject: My big news!

Hi Saskia,

How are you? Hope all is well. So sorry I haven't written for a while, but I've been pretty busy with school work. Anyway, thanks for your invitation to visit this summer. I've had a word with Mum and Dad and they said they'll think about it. I'll let you know as soon as they make their minds up.

So, my big news is that I've entered a national essay writing competition. It's being run by *The Daily Telegraph* and they want readers to nominate a family hero. You just have to choose a relative and answer why they deserve to win an award. It was really easy for me because Jennie, my older sister, has always been my hero. I think I told you she has autism, which means life can be pretty tough for her at times. However, when she isn't trying to find ways of being able to cope better with her everyday challenges, she's working to help others understand more about the condition. For example, she spoke for 20 minutes in a school assembly last week about what it's like to be autistic. It wasn't an easy thing for her to do, but it was amazing to see the reaction of the other students. I was so proud of her. I've attached a photo of her in the assembly. She also spends most of her weekends working with a charity that offers support to children who have autistic siblings (like me). I don't suppose I'll win, but it felt good just to sit down and put into writing just how amazing Jennie is.

I promise I'll let you know if I do win though. Actually, the closing date for entries is the 30th, I believe, so if you want to write in about anyone, you've still got time. Let me know if you do decide to enter.

Love,

Lola

2 ANALYSE **Read through the first paragraph again. Which of these things does Lola do?**

refers to her friend's suggestion ☐
gives reasons for the delay in her reply ☐
tells her friend what's been happening in her life ☐
responds to her friend's news ☐
enquires how her friend is ☐

3 Read through the email again and complete Lola's notes.

Family hero: _____
(my _____)
Jennie's challenge: living with
_____
What Jennie wants: _____
Examples of how she does this:
_____
_____

4 PLAN **Imagine you are Saskia. You have decided to enter the competition. You are going to write to Lola and tell her who you have chosen and why. Look again at her email and think about how you want to respond. Make notes.**

5 PRODUCE **Write your email to Lola (220–260 words). Use your notes from Exercise 4. Write your own checklist.**

✔ **CHECKLIST**

☐ _____
☐ _____
☐ _____
☐ _____
☐ _____

🎧 LISTENING

1 🔊 1.01 **Listen to the conversation. What is the relationship between the people?**

A They're cousins.   B They're best friends.   C They're siblings.

2 **Circle the word to describe each person.**

1 Grace: *self-centred /*
rebellious / traditional

2 Lucas: *insecure /*
demanding / self-centred

3 Lily: *respectful /*
unconventional / insecure

3 🔊 1.01 **Listen again and mark the sentences T (true), F (false) or DS (doesn't say).**

1 Lucas is 18 today. ☐

2 Lucas is the youngest of the three speakers. ☐

3 Grace had her ears pierced on her 16th birthday. ☐

4 Grace's parents didn't mind her having her ears pierced. ☐

5 Lily isn't going to have her ears pierced on her 15th birthday. ☐

6 Lucas doesn't always annoy his sisters. ☐

4 **Look at the lines from the conversation. What emotive technique is being used to add emphasis? Look on page 15 of the Student's Book to help you.**

1 You're all grown up now, aren't you?
_____

2 You must be joking!
_____

3 Since when did I have to ask my little brother for permission? _____

4 You really enjoyed not doing what people in authority wanted you to do, didn't you?
_____

5 I don't understand. I really don't.
_____

6 Honestly, you are still the worst for sharing. The worst. _____

7 You do get on my nerves sometimes.
_____

DIALOGUE

1 **Put the dialogue in order.**

☐ Freya What do you mean? Why would I want to go there?

☐ Freya You know exactly what: my new trainers. What have you done with them?

☐ Freya I will and if I find them, there will be trouble.

☐ Freya I'm sorry but I don't believe you. You're always taking my things without asking.

☐ Freya So you won't mind if I take a look in your room then, will you?

1 Freya OK, Freya, where are they?

☐ Orla No, I won't. Go ahead. Be my guest.

☐ Orla Where's what?

☐ Orla Well this time I'm not guilty. Sorry to disappoint you.

☐ Orla But before you waste your time, you might want to check in Lucy's room first.

☐ Orla Nothing. I've done nothing with your stupid trainers.

☐ Orla Just that maybe your favourite baby sister has something that belongs to you. I'm not always the problem, you know.

2 **Choose one of the following and write a ten-line dialogue. Use at least three examples of emotive language.**

- You see your brother/sister in town wearing your new leather jacket. They didn't ask you before they took it.

- You post a picture of a friend on social media without asking their permission. Your friend notices and is not happy about it.

PRONUNCIATION
Intonation: showing emotions   Go to page 118. 🎧

C1 Advanced

Part 2: Open cloze

1 For questions 1–8, read the text below and think of the word which best fits each gap. Use only one word in each gap. There is an example at the beginning (0).

Cousins

What **(0)** _____is_____ it about cousins that makes them so special? I remember when I was a kid we **(1)** _____ to hang out with our cousins every summer holiday. They really were great times. Now I watch the joy that my **(2)** _____ children experience every time we go and visit my sister and her children. **(3)** _____ five days I hardly see my three boys as they're off exploring and playing with a brand **(4)** _____ set of toys. But what's even more amazing is that I hardly hear them either. Back home I'm called upon at **(5)** _____ three times a day to break up a fight between two of them but when they're with their cousins it's as if they've all suddenly become the best **(6)** _____ friends. There's no arguing. No one seems to get on anyone else's nerves. And I rarely have to have words with any of them. There are often a few tears in the back of the car when we have to leave and promises that we **(7)** _____ be back to visit soon. Ten minutes later as I'm pulling onto the motorway the fighting begins. It's amazing **(8)** _____ quickly normal service is resumed.

2 For questions 1–8, read the text below and think of the word which best fits each gap. Use only one word in each gap. There is an example at the beginning (0).

Animal families

Family relationships play **(0)** _____such_____ an important part in the human world, from shaping our individual personalities to providing inspiration for much of our storytelling. Psychologists have dedicated their lives to the subject and hundreds of books have **(1)** _____ written on the topic. However, when it comes to the animal kingdom, not nearly as **(2)** _____ research has been done. In his book *Sisters and Brothers: Sibling Relationships in the Animal World*, author Steve Jenkins takes a look **(3)** _____ some of the more interesting examples of sibling behaviour in different species of animals. Perhaps **(4)** _____ of the biggest differences is that while multiple births are rare in humans, they are commonplace for many animals. It **(5)** _____ be quite unusual for a cat to give birth to only one kitten. As a consequence, a lot of newly born animals find they are part of a large family **(6)** _____ the day they are born. This can often lead to quite cruel consequences with weaker siblings dying from **(7)** _____ unable to fight for the food that they need. **(8)** _____ some extreme cases they can be deliberately killed by a brother or sister.

2 SWEET DREAMS

Grammar video

▶04

 GRAMMAR

Past tenses with hypothetical meaning → SB p.22

1 ★☆☆ **Circle the correct option.**

1 It's time we *stop* / *stopped* talking and did something about it.

2 I wish we *doesn't* / *didn't* have so much homework to do.

3 I'd prefer *to text* / *text* him rather than give him a call.

4 If only our house *was* / *is* a bit bigger. I'd love to have my own bedroom.

5 I'd prefer he *say* / *said* sorry in person.

6 It's time *turn* / *to turn* off your computer and do something else.

7 I wish I *knew* / *know* the answer to that question. I really wish I *do* / *did*.

8 If only I *have* / *had* enough money to buy a new tablet.

2 ★★☆ **Complete the sentences with the correct form of the verbs.**

1 It's time you _____ to bed. You can't stop yawning. (go)

2 I wish this bed _____ so hard. It's really uncomfortable. (not be)

3 If only I _____ so much coffee. I would be able to get to sleep more easily. (not drink)

4 I'd prefer it if you _____ talking. I'm trying to get to sleep. (stop)

5 If only the neighbours _____ their music so loud. I can't get to sleep. (not play)

6 I wish I _____ stop thinking about my exam tomorrow. (can)

7 It's time we _____ a new bed for you. This one's about to collapse. (buy)

8 I'd prefer it if we _____ the light on. It's stopping me from getting to sleep. (not keep)

3 ★★☆ **Rewrite the sentences using the word in brackets.**

0 You need to get up now. (time)

_____*It's time you got up now.*_____

1 It would be nice to live in the countryside. (wish)

_____

2 I think we should leave half an hour earlier. (prefer)

_____

3 It's 2 pm and I haven't had lunch yet. That's why I'm so hungry! (time)

_____

4 I'd like it to stop raining now! (only)

_____

5 My choice would be to walk to the party. (prefer)

_____

4 ★★★ **Complete the sentences with your own ideas.**

1 I'd prefer to _____ _____

3 If only _____ _____

2 I wish _____ _____

4 It's time _____ _____

Adverbs for modifying comparatives

→ SB p.25

5 ★☆☆ **Complete the dialogue with the phrases in the list. There are three phrases you do not need.**

> a lot | be much | considerably quicker
> far bigger | far more | it's way
> lot more | more complex

Tim So tell me about this book idea of yours. It's a kind of dream dictionary, isn't it?

Alba No, it's ¹_____ exciting than that. Think of it as a dream encyclopedia.

Tim So you use it to find out what your dream might mean.

Alba No, it's ²_____ more useful than that. Yes, you can find out about your dream, but it also gives you advice on how to act on this information.

Tim So, I dream about a cat and then I look up 'cat' in your book and it tells me what my dream means and what to do about it?

Alba No, it's considerably ³_____ than that. You'll need to look at the context of your dream, too.

Tim But how are you going to fit all of this in a book?

Alba It's going to be ⁴_____ than just a book. It's going to be a series of 20 books.

Tim Really? And you're going to write all this in a year?

Alba A year? No, it's going to be ⁵_____ than that. I hope to have it finished by May.

Tim But we're already in March!

6 ★★☆ **Rewrite the sentences to modify the comparative using the words in brackets. Sometimes this will change the meaning of the sentence.**

1 She is as talented as her younger sister. (nowhere near)

_____

2 The Eiffel Tower is taller than I thought it would be. (far)

_____

3 It is cheaper to take the bus than the train. (way)

_____

4 That rollercoaster is as scary as it looks. (nothing like)

_____

5 This exam is more difficult than the one you did last week. (significantly)

_____

6 This situation is more serious than we first thought. (drastically)

_____

7 ★★★ **Complete the sentences with your own ideas.**

1 _____ is far more exciting than I thought it would be.

2 _____ is notably more difficult than when my parents were young.

3 _____ is significantly more interesting than playing computer games.

4 _____ is way easier than my teacher said it would be.

5 _____ is much more enjoyable than watching TV.

6 _____ is nowhere near as boring as _____ .

7 _____ is not nearly as complicated as _____ .

8 _____ is a lot more disgusting than _____ .

GET IT *RIGHT!*

as … as …

Learners often omit *as* in *as … as* phrases when using modifiers.

✓ *Rob is nowhere near as clever a builder as Jason.*

✗ *Rob is nowhere ~~near clever a builder as~~ Jason.*

Rewrite the sentences using *as … as* and *not nearly, nowhere near* or *nothing like*.

0 I'm surprised, but you are much more surprised than me.
 I'm not nearly as surprised as you.
 I'm nowhere near as surprised as you.
 I'm nothing like as surprised as you.

1 My dream was strange but yours was far stranger!

_____

_____

2 Some countries don't value the importance of sleep while other nations value it much more.

_____

_____

3 Working in this office isn't very interesting. My dream job is much more interesting.

_____

_____

4 Brazilians take naps far more than the Japanese.

_____

_____

5 Sleepwalking is much less mysterious than it seems.

_____

_____

VOCABULARY
Sleep → SB p.22

1 ★☆☆ **Match the phrases (1–8) with the definitions (a–h).**

1 take a nap ☐
2 lie in ☐
3 a light sleeper ☐
4 fast asleep ☐
5 snore loudly ☐
6 nod off ☐
7 fall asleep ☐
8 under the covers ☐

a to stay in bed later than usual in the morning
b someone who is easily woken up
c to breathe in a very noisy way while you are sleeping
d to start to sleep
e to begin sleeping, especially not intentionally
f in bed, under the bed sheets
g to have a short sleep, especially during the day
h sleeping deeply

2 ★★☆ **Complete the text with the phrases from Exercise 1.**

I like sleeping. You might say it's one of my hobbies. At bedtime I always ¹_____ really easily. I like to get at least eight hours a night if I can and sometimes I'll ²_____ in the afternoon. I've also been known to ³_____ on the school bus on the way home. That can be a bit embarrassing.
I'm not really a big fan of early mornings. That's why I like the weekends so much when I have a chance to ⁴_____ (if Mum and Dad let me, that is). During the week, I have to get up at 7 am, which is really hard and sometimes my parents have to practically pull me out from ⁵_____ to get me out of bed.
I share a bedroom with my twin sister. She likes her sleep, too, and sometimes she ⁶_____ really _____ . Luckily I'm not a ⁷_____ , so I don't really hear her. I'm usually ⁸_____ by the time she goes to bed anyway!

3 ★★☆ **Circle the correct options.**

1 I sometimes forget to set my alarm and *lie in / oversleep* in the mornings.
2 My brother doesn't get *full / enough* sleep – he plays computer games until late.
3 I think it's really bad to *skip / lack* sleep when studying for exams.
4 We're suffering from a *lack / need* of sleep.
5 I like to try and *get / find* seven hours' sleep a night.

4 ★★★ **Write a short paragraph about your sleeping habits. Write about …**

• how much you sleep
• where you sleep
• weekday mornings vs. weekend mornings.

Idioms with *sleep* and *dream* → SB p.25

5 ★★☆ **Put the words in order to make phrases.**

1 dreams / my / it's / wildest / beyond
_____

2 something / dream / that / of / I'd / doing / never / like
_____

3 a / true / come / dream / it's
_____

4 my / to / get / need / sleep / beauty / I
_____

5 sleep / it / lose / over / don't
_____

6 dreams / your / in
_____

7 me / it / on / sleep / let
_____

8 my / dream / it's / job
_____

6 ★★☆ **Use the phrases from Exercise 5 to complete the dialogues. There is sometimes more than one possible answer.**

1 A So how do you feel about being chosen to sing a solo at the prom?
  B _____

2 A Alfie, you didn't eat my chocolate bar that was in the fridge, did you?
  B Me? _____

3 A I'm a bit worried about my driving test tomorrow.
  B Well, _____ . I'm sure you'll be fine.

4 A What – you're off to bed already? It's only 9 o'clock.
  B I know, but _____ .

5 A So, what do you say? Shall we go camping this weekend?
  B I'm not sure. _____ and I'll give you an answer in the morning.

6 A Do you think Jack Munro would go to the cinema with me?
  B _____ .

7 A So, what's it like being a pilot?
  B _____ .
  It's perfect.

8 A How does it feel being reunited with your long-lost twin sister?
  B _____ .
  Something I thought would never happen.

REFERENCE

IDIOMS WITH *SLEEP* AND *DREAM*

VOCABULARY EXTRA

1 Circle the correct preposition for each phrasal verb.

1 *sleep on / through:*
to continue sleeping and not to wake up by a noise or an activity

2 *sleep off / over:*
to sleep at someone else's house for a night

3 *sleep in / out:*
to sleep later in the morning than you usually do

4 *sleep through / out:*
to sleep outdoors

5 *sleep off / on*
(something): to go to sleep so that you will feel better when you wake up

2 Complete the dialogues with phrasal verbs from Exercise 1.

1 A Shall we _____ in our tent tonight?
  B Maybe. Let's check the weather first!

2 A I don't feel very well. I have a headache. I can't meet you.
  B Why don't you go to bed and _____ your headache. We can meet tomorrow.

3 A Do you want to go to the late-night movie on Friday?
  B Good idea. We can _____ the next morning.

4 A Did you hear the storm last night? It was so loud.
  B No. I _____ everything! Nothing wakes me up.

5 A Oh, no. I've missed the last bus.
  B Don't worry. You can come and _____ at my house tonight if you want.

3 Complete the sentences so they are true for you.

1 I always sleep in _____ .
2 _____ is my favourite place to sleep out because _____ .
3 When I have an important decision to make, I usually sleep on _____ .

It's no secret that getting a good night's sleep is an important part of leading a healthy lifestyle. Of course, not everyone needs the same amount of sleep, but what is generally agreed on is that the quality (rather than quantity) of your sleep time can have a huge influence on your well-being. As many doctors agree, one way of ensuring that quality is to look closely at your pre-sleep routine. Here is how some of the world's most important people go about doing this.

Former US president Barack Obama has referred to himself as a night owl. It's not always easy to find time to relax when you're in charge of one of the world's largest economies. He would often be discussing business until 11 pm, although he would always try and have dinner with his family and put his children to bed before getting back to work.

Ariana Huffington is the co-founder of the American newspaper, *The Huffington Post*. However, a few years ago, she collapsed due to a lack of sleep. She knew then that it was time to change her sleeping habits. She suggests avoiding caffeine after 2 pm and she stops using electronic devices half an hour before she goes to bed. She prefers her bedroom to be dark, quiet and cool.

In the world of technology, the CEO of Apple Inc, Tim Cook, runs one of the US's most profitable businesses. He is usually fast asleep by 9.30 pm and often gets up before the sun rises. Surprisingly, the first thing he does when he wakes up at 4.30 am is to spend about an hour reading emails or comments from Apple users. He feels that it's important to focus on users of his company's products and listen to their views. After that, he goes to the gym for an hour, which helps him reduce his stress levels. As the rest of California begins to wake up, he is ready to start reading his work emails!

The singer and actor J-Lo claims that getting a good night's sleep is one of her priorities in life, because it helps her to stay healthy. She likes to get at least eight hours' sleep a night despite being the mother to twins. She rests when she can in the evening and she knows that this is important, so she can be the best mother for her children and the best professional she can be. However, that isn't her ideal schedule. If she could choose her own schedule, she would stay up until 4 am or 5 am and then go to bed in the late morning! Maybe next time when you're complaining about getting up early, J-Lo will just be going to bed!

📖 READING

1 Read the article and choose the best title for it.

A Good sleeping habits

B The night-time secrets of success

C Achieve more with a good night's sleep

2 Read the article again and answer the questions.

Who ...

1 didn't use to get enough sleep? _____

2 would always try and eat an evening meal with their family? _____

3 has an ideal schedule that is different from their current sleep schedule? _____

4 would often go back to work until very late after doing other things? _____

5 knows that getting enough sleep helps with their family and professional responsibilities? _____

6 checks emails as soon as they get up? _____

7 stops doing certain things before they go to bed? _____

8 goes to the gym before they start their day's work? _____

3 CRITICAL THINKING Read the suggestions below. Which ones do you think are helpful for having a good night's sleep? Give reasons.

1 Watch YouTube videos until you fall asleep.

2 Switch off all electronic devices at least half an hour before you go to bed.

3 Take your phone to bed and charge it by your bed overnight.

4 Drink lots of water during the day.

5 Have a big meal after 10 pm.

6 Read a book or listen to some music before you go to bed.

4 Write a short paragraph about what you do to get a good night's sleep.

_____

_____

_____

_____

Writing a proposal

1   **INPUT** **Read the proposal. What do the students want?**

   A   more physical exercise lessons for all students
   B   more time for students to use electronic devices
   C   more exercise during the school day

Subject: a proposal from Year 12 students to introduce compulsory physical exercise during the school day

The principal aim of this proposal is to evaluate the benefits of physical exercise and to recommend the introduction of compulsory physical exercise for all students during the school day.

According to a recent survey, we all need about 30 minutes of regular exercise a day, five days a week. Exercise not only benefits our general health and well-being; it helps us sleep better. Furthermore, it also improves concentration and reduces stress.

With an increase in the usage of electronic devices at home and in school and the amount of time we spend sitting in front of screens or behind desks in the classroom, we feel this is leading to a less active school community.

In a number of other schools in the area, compulsory physical exercise has been introduced during the school day. Surprisingly, students who did the classes scored higher in tests and exams and were happier and less stressed than those who hadn't done them.

We understand that not everyone is the same, so we are proposing different 30-minute activities at different times of the school day. Early morning Wake Up and Shake Up; Lunchtime Song and Dance and After-School Yoga. Students choose one activity each day.

We strongly recommend that the headteacher and the staff conduct a trial programme of offering the classes for one month. We suggest that the effects and impact of the exercise on students' results, mood, behaviour and sleep should be monitored and if these are shown to be beneficial, the exercise programmes should become a compulsory part of the school day.

2   **ANALYSE** **Read the proposal again. Answer the questions.**

   1   What are the health benefits of exercise?
   _____

   2   Why do the students feel people are doing less exercise?
   _____

   3   What evidence from other schools do students give to support their idea?
   _____

   4   What type of classes are students proposing?
   _____

WRITING TIP: A PROPOSAL

- Introduction: start by saying what it is about.
- Paragraph 1: outline the background information, using statistical evidence if relevant.
- Main body: your ideas on what should be done to improve this situation, pointing out all the benefits from the proposed course of action.
- Final paragraph: a short paragraph to emphasise why you feel your proposal should be adopted.

3   **Complete the examples of useful language with phrases from the proposal.**

   Ways of introducing the reason for the proposal
   - The main purpose …
   - The intention of …
   - The prime objective of …
   1   _____

   Introducing statistical information
   - The results of a recent survey suggest …
   - A scientific study has shown …
   - The findings of the latest opinion polls are …
   2   _____

   Ways of putting across your opinion
   - It is our belief …
   - In our opinion …
   3   _____
   4   _____

4   **PLAN** **You want to introduce compulsory exercise classes to your school. Add two more points to each list.**

   Benefits:
   - It will help students to get fitter.
   - _____
   - _____

   Points to consider:
   - How will teachers know if a student has done a class?
   - _____
   - _____

5   **PRODUCE** **Write a proposal (220–260 words) to your headteacher recommending compulsory exercise classes for students at your school. Use your points from Exercise 4 and the information in the Tip box to help. Write your own checklist.**

✓ CHECKLIST

   ☐ _____
   ☐ _____

🎧 LISTENING

1 🔊 2.01 **Listen to the conversations. What's keeping these people up at night? Write the names *Bruno*, *Ingrid* or *Olivia* under the pictures. There is one extra picture.**

1 _____

3 _____

2 _____

4 _____

2 🔊 2.01 **Listen again and mark the sentences T (true) or F (false).**

Conversation 1

1 The police didn't do anything about Bruno's complaint. ☐

2 Bruno has decided that earplugs are his last chance of getting a good night's sleep. ☐

Conversation 2

3 Ingrid's had problems with dogs barking in the past. ☐

4 Paul thinks Ingrid may have a bird in her attic. ☐

Conversation 3

5 Olivia's brother has had a snoring problem for a few years. ☐

6 Megan defends Olivia's brother. ☐

3 **Complete the advice with the missing suggestions. Then listen again and check.**

Conversation 1

1 Well, you might want to consider

_____ .

Conversation 2

2 I recommend _____ to come and have a look.

Conversation 3

3 Well try not to _____ .

4 I find that _____ is a good way of falling asleep.

DIALOGUE

1 **Complete the dialogue with the missing lines (1–6).**

Ruby Hi Jamie. How's your science project going?

Jamie ☐

Ruby Two weeks!

Jamie ☐

Ruby Well, try not to think about it too much. It'll be worth it when it's finished.

Jamie ☐

Ruby And while you're doing it, you're learning loads of new things, right?

Jamie ☐

Ruby Poor you. You might want to take a few more naps during the day.

Jamie ☐

Ruby A lack of sleep won't help you. I recommend taking a nap at some point every day!

Jamie ☐

1 That's a good idea. Why didn't I think of that?

2 I suppose I am. I'm not getting much sleep though. I have to check some of the experiments during the night.

3 I certainly hope it will.

4 I think I'll need about another two weeks to finish it.

5 I might just do that. Thanks, Ruby!

6 Yes, the experiments are taking ages.

2 **Write a dialogue (8–10 lines) between someone who has a sleeping problem and a friend who is trying to give them some advice.**

> **PRONUNCIATION**
> Different ways of pronouncing *c* and *g*
> Go to page 118.

C1 Advanced

EXAM GUIDE:

Part 1 of the Advanced Reading and Use of English exam is designed to test your knowledge of vocabulary. Unlike Part 2 (the open cloze), you will not be tested on grammatical structures. Areas of vocabulary that commonly feature include: idiomatic language (including phrasal verbs), fixed phrases, words with similar meaning and collocations.

- Look carefully at the meaning of the sentence which the words are in. Sometimes you will also need to consider the sentence after. Make sure that the word you choose makes sense in the sentence.
- Look carefully at the words immediately before and after the gap. These will give you clues as to whether the word is part of a fixed phrase.
- Finally, if you have time, read through the whole passage again with your choices in place. Does the text make sense with the words that you have chosen?

A CURE FOR SNORING

I'm what you might describe as a **(0)** _____light_____ sleeper. I'll wake up at the slightest noise and usually find it difficult to get back to sleep. **(1)** _____ I rarely get a good night's sleep, meaning I'm often moody and irritable throughout the day. I've also been known to nod **(2)** _____ at my desk, much to the amusement of my colleagues. More often than not, it is my husband's snoring that **(3)** _____ my sleeplessness. Although I'm usually fast asleep when he comes to bed, it's never long before his snoring **(4)** _____ my sleep and I'm wide awake not long after.

Therefore, when I read about a miracle cure for people who snore promising a 100 percent success guarantee it was something **(5)** _____ my wildest dreams. My husband was a little unsure, but then he denies that he has a problem in the first place. The treatment involves the insertion of a small appliance that sits between your teeth and **(6)** _____ a blockage of the soft tissue at the back of your throat, which is what causes the snoring. It's simple, easy to fit and not **(7)** _____ expensive. That final consideration is what has led my husband to reluctantly agree to **(8)** _____ it a go. Hopefully, this time next week my sleeping problem will have been solved.

1 **For questions 1–8, read the text below and decide which answer (A, B, C or D) best fits each gap. There is an example at the beginning (0).**

0 A weak	**(B)** light	**C** heavy	**D** fragile
1 A Contrary	**B** Resultantly	**C** Consequently	**D** However
2 A off	**B** through	**C** over	**D** out
3 A begins	**B** makes	**C** triggers	**D** generates
4 A intrudes	**B** interferes	**C** interrupts	**D** infects
5 A further	**B** afar	**C** outside	**D** beyond
6 A avoids	**B** prevents	**C** causes	**D** cleans
7 A offensively	**B** shamefully	**C** outrageously	**D** disgracefully
8 A try	**B** have	**C** offer	**D** give

CONSOLIDATION

🎧 LISTENING

1 🔊 2.03 **Listen to Lydia talking to Paul about being the eldest child. Which of these complaints does she have?**

☐ She can never do well enough at school for her parents.

☐ Her parents expect her to help out in the house too much.

☐ Her parents give her younger sister more freedom.

☐ Her parents expect her to act more maturely.

☐ She's not allowed to go to parties.

☐ Her parents think she treats her younger sister badly.

2 🔊 2.03 **Listen again and mark the sentences T (true), F (false) or DS (doesn't say).**

1 Lydia's favourite subject at school is PE. ☐

2 Lydia feels that her parents have forgotten what it's like to be young. ☐

3 She wants her parents to tell her that they're proud of her. ☐

4 Lauren is two years younger than Lydia. ☐

5 Lydia's parents accuse her of not doing what is expected. ☐

6 Paul doesn't really sympathise with Lydia. ☐

7 Paul is one of three brothers. ☐

8 Paul often sticks up for his brother. ☐

Ⓖ GRAMMAR

3 **Rewrite or correct the sentences using the word in brackets.**

1 I don't know why I said that. (honestly)
   _____

2 If we didn't have to go to school today. (only)
   _____

3 That was the worst game of football ever played. (surely)
   _____

4 It's quicker to walk there than to take the car. (far)
   _____

5 My brother is trying to get me in trouble. (always)
   _____

6 I'd prefer take a break and finish this tomorrow. (to)
   _____

7 The test was nowhere as difficult as I thought it would be. (near)
   _____

8 We used be friends until he started going out with my sister. (to)
   _____

🄰z VOCABULARY

4 **Match the sentence halves.**

1 If you're feeling tired, ☐

2 If you don't need to get up early tomorrow, ☐

3 If your brother snores so loudly, ☐

4 If you're a light sleeper, ☐

5 If she's getting on your nerves, ☐

6 If you're getting bullied at school, ☐

7 If she's already said sorry, ☐

8 If you're scared of making things worse, ☐

a why don't you sleep in a different room?

b why don't you avoid her for a while?

c why don't you just let her be?

d why don't you lie in?

e then don't say anything to her.

f why don't you have a word with your teacher?

g why don't you take a quick nap before dinner?

h why don't you wear earplugs?

5 **Match the words in the list with what the people say.**

demanding | insecure | outgoing | rebellious
respectful | self-centred | traditional | unconventional

1 'I love travelling by bus. There's always someone new to talk to.'
   _____

2 'I don't care what Dad says. I'm going to that party tonight.'
   _____

3 'I'm not having a birthday party in case no one comes.'
   _____

4 'The audience is obviously here just to see me.'
   _____

5 'I believe that a man should always open a door for a lady.'
   _____

6 'Get me a glass of water – now!'
   _____

7 'You can laugh if you want, but I've always put sugar on my pasta.'
   _____

8 'We must be quiet when we go into this building.'
   _____

DIALOGUE

6 Complete the dialogue with the phrases in the list. There are two you do not need to use.

> always taking | consider getting
> did you | didn't you | light
> rebellious | self-centred | tell me

Alice ¹_____ you haven't taken my alarm clock again.

Jody My phone stopped working, and I need to get up really early tomorrow.

Alice So you thought you could just take mine, ²_____ ?

Jody Well, you never use it. You're a really ³_____ sleeper.

Alice That's not the point. It's mine and you should ask. You're ⁴_____ my things without asking.

Jody Someone's in a bad mood today. You might want to ⁵_____ a bit more sleep.

Alice Actually, I'm not. I'm just tired of you being so ⁶_____ .

 ## READING

7 Read the article and answer the questions.

1 What might be the most natural way to sleep?

_____

2 How did beds change in the Neolithic period?

_____

3 How did people sleep in 8,000 BCE?

_____

4 How did beds and mattresses change in the Middle Ages?

_____

5 What would people in the Renaissance period do when they were awake in the middle of the night?

_____

6 Why did sleeping patterns change in the UK during the industrial revolution?

_____

7 How did electricity change sleeping patterns?

_____

A short history of sleep

One in three people suffers from a lack of sleep, including staying asleep during the night. Sleeping like this often makes people feel stressed. There is evidence to suggest that being awake during the night is not abnormal and that historically, rest was divided into periods. It may in fact be the most natural and healthy way to sleep.

Neolithic era
In this period, there weren't bright night skies and the threat of predators meant that Neolithic people went to bed a few hours after dusk. They made an effort to make their bed space more comfortable, unlike their Stone Age ancestors who used to use straw on the floor as a bed. For the first time, beds started to become raised surfaces.

8,000 BCE
Archaeologists have discovered ancient circular sleeping spaces that look more like nests than beds. This type of bed suggests that people at this time preferred to sleep curled up like babies and not on their sides or backs.

1300s to 1600s
This was the Middle Ages and conditions for rich and poor were often described as damp, smelly and dirty. There were big increases in population and living areas became crowded and over-populated. However, sleeping became a lot more comfortable with beds and mattresses filled with straw or feathers.

The Renaissance period
Suddenly, the rough cloth and straw mattresses were covered in velvet and silk for rich people and beds were far more luxurious than ever before. During this time, there is evidence of people having a first and then a second sleep. Between the sleeps, there was a peaceful time of being awake in the middle of the night. Unlike today, people didn't use to worry about this; instead they would use the time to read or even visit friends in the middle of the night!

The industrial revolution
In the UK, as working patterns changed, so did sleeping patterns. With rigid factory schedules, people could no longer enjoy periods of rest between sleeping. People began to sleep in a single cycle without waking up from this point.

19th century
The invention of electricity and street lights changed sleeping patterns completely. Light became one of the most important factors regulating sleep and now with the ability to control light through artificial means, sleep patterns changed. It was during this time that doctors recommended one single period of sleep instead of two separate ones.

 ## WRITING

8 Think about your sleep this week. Write a paragraph (200–220 words) about it. Include …

- how much sleep you had; which nights you slept well / badly
- activities you did during the day and before you went to bed
- any factors that affected your sleep positively or negatively

3 LUCKY FOR SOME?

Grammar video ▶07

⊙ GRAMMAR
Mixed conditionals (review) → SB p.32

1 ★☆☆ **Match the sentence halves.**

1 If Katya were a more careful driver ☐
2 I'd be at home by now ☐
3 Jeremy wouldn't be embarrassed ☐
4 If I hadn't watched the news last night ☐
5 If Mayumi hadn't gone to the beach in Rio ☐
6 Theresa would probably be acting in the theatre now ☐
7 We wouldn't be so unhappy now ☐
8 If Jared paid more attention ☐

a I wouldn't know about the plane crash.
b she wouldn't be married to a Brazilian.
c if I hadn't missed the last bus.
d if she hadn't been late for that audition.
e if we hadn't lost that last match.
f she wouldn't have had that accident.
g he wouldn't have missed the turning and got lost.
h if he hadn't tripped and fallen over on the dance floor.

2 ★★☆ **Complete the gaps with _were / weren't, would / wouldn't_ and _had / hadn't_.**

1 Laura _____ be a top gymnast if she _____ started training very young. She was only four when she began.
2 If Ben _____ read the news, he _____ know the buses were on strike and he _____ be standing waiting at the bus stop at the moment.
3 Skye finds learning French difficult. If she _____ been born in France, she _____ need to study French now.
4 If he _____ better at science, Nico _____ have won the quiz show.
5 Monica _____ have a bandage on her foot if she _____ tripped over the cat and broken her ankle.
6 Denny is over two metres tall. If he _____ , he _____ have started to play basketball.
7 Miranda _____ have been able to reach the top shelf if she _____ taller.
8 Esther _____ be so nervous about the exam if she _____ paid more attention in class.

3 ★★☆ **Complete the sentences with the correct form of the verbs in brackets.**

1 If I _____ (not spend) so much money on that computer last month, I _____ (be) in Spain on holiday now.
2 I _____ (not be) hungry now if my friends _____ (wake) me up in time for breakfast.
3 If my dad _____ (be) younger, he _____ (go) to the rock concert last night.
4 I _____ (not have) to hurry to get things ready for my party now if I _____ (not fall) asleep after lunch.
5 If I _____ (accept) that invitation to her party, I _____ (be) at her flat in London now.
6 I _____ (not need) to work so hard now if I _____ (study) a lot more last term.
7 I _____ (feel) very guilty now if I _____ (forget) my mother's birthday, so I'm really happy that I remembered!
8 Ruben hasn't phoned me, but if he _____ (not miss) the flight last night, he _____ (be) here now.

4 ★★★ **Complete the sentences so they are true for you. Use mixed conditionals.**

1 If I wasn't studying English now, I _____ _____
2 I wouldn't be _____ _____
3 If I had _____ _____
4 If I hadn't _____ _____
5 I would _____ _____
6 If I were _____ _____

Alternatives to *if*   → SB p.35

5 ★★☆ **Cross out the word or words which do NOT fit.**

0 We can go in my car ~~otherwise~~ / as long as / ~~unless~~ we share the cost of petrol.

1 I wouldn't interrupt Mum now *unless* / *if* / *otherwise* you want her to get really angry.

2 *Suppose* / *Imagine* / *As long as* you could visit another planet, where would you go?

3 Eat your soup now, *suppose* / *unless* / *otherwise* it'll get cold.

4 *Unless* / *If* / *Otherwise* you can't get to the front of the crowd, you won't see much of the parade.

5 Of course you can borrow my book, *as long as* / *unless* / *provided that* you don't lose it.

6 *Imagine* / *Provided that* / *Suppose* you get there early, there will be plenty of space to sit.

6 ★★☆ **Complete the dialogue with the words and phrases in the list.**

> as long as | if | imagine | otherwise
> provided that | suppose | unless

Maisie My brother won't eat vegetables ¹_____ they're green.

Dan Why?

Maisie He says green is his lucky colour, so ²_____ Mum gives him green vegetables, he's OK.

Dan ³_____ she gave him carrots, what would he do?

Maisie He'd refuse to eat them.

Dan ⁴_____ she could dye them green – what then?

Maisie Yeah, that might work. But only if she told him they were special beans or something, ⁵_____ he wouldn't eat them.

Dan Well, ⁶_____ that's the only thing he's picky about eating, then that's a good thing! His lucky colour could be brown – he would only eat chocolate!

Maisie Well, I suppose you're right, ⁷_____ he grows out of it soon. I'm sick of only eating green vegetables at home.

7 ★★☆ **Rewrite the rules using the words in brackets.**

Rules for college students

1 You can come in after 11 pm. But tell the porter when you leave.

2 You mustn't leave your bicycle on the lawn if you are not going out immediately.

3 You can have a wake-up call in the morning. Just tell the night porter.

4 You can use the kitchen, but please leave it clean and tidy.

5 Keep your key safe. If you don't, you might get locked out.

6 Please only use the college phone in an emergency.

1 (as long as) _____
2 (unless) _____
3 (if) _____
4 (provided that) _____
5 (otherwise) _____
6 (unless) _____

GET IT *RIGHT!*

unless

Learners often use *unless* with a negative verb form when they should use a positive form.

✓ *Unless you do your homework, you can't play your game.*

✗ *Unless you ~~don't~~ do your homework, you can't play your game.*

Tick (✓) the sentences which are correct. Rewrite the incorrect ones.

1 Unless you don't play the lottery, you don't have a chance of winning it!

_____

2 We can deliver it next week, unless you need it tomorrow.

_____

3 Juan's going to miss the beginning of the film unless he doesn't turn up in the next two minutes.

_____

4 I will take you up on your offer unless you've changed your mind.

_____

5 Sophia never travels on a Friday unless she absolutely doesn't have to.

_____

PRONUNCIATION
Unstressed words in connected speech   Go to page 118.

VOCABULARY
Phrasal verbs

→ SB p.32

1 ★★☆ **Complete the crossword.**

Across

2 Are you going to _____ on at the café or find a new Saturday job?

4 It's a funny feeling when you _____ to after fainting.

5 Why didn't you _____ up the phone earlier? I tried calling three times.

6 I can't believe Libby _____ down the job. It looked really interesting.

7 Can you help me? My dog _____ away and I can't find her.

Down

1 Be careful! Don't _____ over that chair.

2 What time do we need to _____ off for the airport?

3 The plans all _____ out really well for Gemma's surprise party.

6 I think we should _____ back now. The weather looks awful.

2 ★★☆ **Complete the sentences with a phrasal verb in the correct form.**

1 I'm so happy that it all _____ for you and you got the job.

2 If Tom doesn't _____ , we can message him.

3 I think the chicken _____ because it saw the fox.

4 When I _____ after fainting, I saw three faces staring at me.

5 We _____ at school next year. We're not leaving.

6 Sadly, the climbers _____ before they reached the summit.

7 They _____ three hours ago. They should have arrived by now.

8 I _____ the job offer. I'm going to start my own business.

Expressions with *luck*

→ SB p.33

3 ★☆☆ **Complete the phrases with one word.**

1 Oh dear, _____ luck.

2 You're _____ your luck.

3 And I thought: it's _____ my luck.

4 She was _____ luck.

5 They didn't _____ me any luck.

6 It's just _____ luck.

7 As luck would _____ it …

8 _____ luck next time.

4 ★★☆ **Complete the dialogues with the phrases from Exercise 3.**

0 A I just missed the bus!
   B ___1___ !

1 A You've never played this before – and you won?
   B I know. Sorry! _____

2 A So your sister met the rock star?
   B Yes. They were staying at the same hotel. _____

3 A Did you try to buy a ticket for the concert?
   B Yes. But they had sold out. _____

4 A So your car broke down?
   B Yes. _____ , though, we were very close to a garage.

5 A Dad, can you lend me another £20?
   B Wow. _____

6 A Did you wear your lucky boots for the game?
   B I did. _____ , though. I lost!

7 A I failed my driving test. Again!
   B I'm sorry to hear that. _____

WordWise:
Expressions with *over*

→ SB p.35

5 **Complete the sentences with a phrase from the list.**

> all over | all over again
> fall over | just over | overall

1 My school's _____ a kilometre away, so it's a quick bike ride for me.

2 Their new song is so good that when I'd finished listening to it, I decided to listen to it _____ .

3 The graphics are great, the music is OK and it isn't expensive – so, _____ , it's a good game.

4 I forgot about the bath and there was water _____ the floor.

5 I was so tired, I thought I was going to _____ when I was going up the stairs to bed!

REFERENCE
Phrasal verbs

pick up | set out | stay on | turn back | turn down | turn out | work out

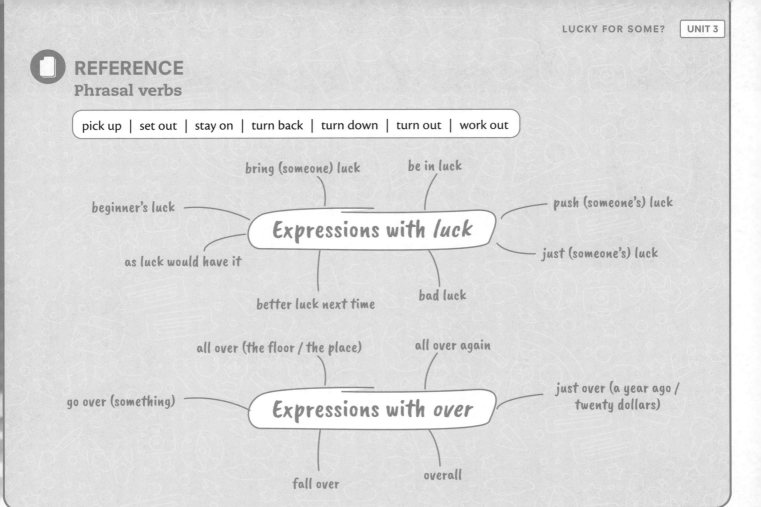

bring (someone) luck

be in luck

beginner's luck

push (someone's) luck

Expressions with luck

just (someone's) luck

as luck would have it

better luck next time

bad luck

all over (the floor / the place)

all over again

go over (something)

Expressions with over

just over (a year ago / twenty dollars)

fall over

overall

VOCABULARY EXTRA

1 Complete the definitions with a verb from the list.

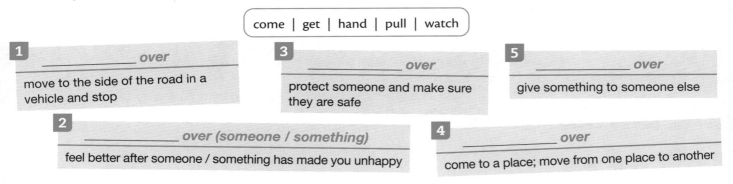

come | get | hand | pull | watch

1 _____ over
move to the side of the road in a vehicle and stop

3 _____ over
protect someone and make sure they are safe

5 _____ over
give something to someone else

2 _____ over (someone / something)
feel better after someone / something has made you unhappy

4 _____ over
come to a place; move from one place to another

2 Complete the dialogue with the correct phrasal verbs from Exercise 1.

A I'm really upset. Libby isn't talking to me.

B Oh dear. What happened?

A I invited her to [1]_____ to my house last night and she refused. She said I was more like a little sister than a friend. She said she had to [2]_____ me all the time.

B That's not very nice.

A I know. Sorry. Can you [3]_____ at the side of the road? I'm going to phone her now.

B I don't think that's a good idea. [4]_____ your phone to me now before you do or say anything silly.

A You sound like my mum! I'm not giving you my phone but you're probably right.

B Try not to think about it anymore. You'll [5]_____ it. I'm sure she'll apologise.

3 Complete the sentences so they are true for you.

1 The next piece of work I have to hand over is … and it's due on …

2 I think it's difficult to get over …

3 The last time I was in a car and it pulled over was …

I can't live without ...

Jody, 17

For me, it's my dream catcher. You've probably seen one hanging from a tree or outside a house or even in a souvenir shop, but mine is in my bedroom. My grandma gave it to me when I was born. I wouldn't know what it was for if my grandma hadn't told me. It's a small wooden hoop covered in threads, they look like a spider's web, and it has long feathers and colourful beads hanging from it. My grandma has Native American heritage and it's a symbol of protection. They are used to protect you when you sleep, especially children. If you have a bad dream, the dreamcatcher catches it. Only good dreams can pass through it and they slide down the feathers to the sleeping person. I'm going to college next year and my dreamcatcher will come, too!

Aarya, 18

I have this dolphin necklace. My grandpa gave it to me and I wear it all the time. He was an Italian fisherman and he would never go out on his boat without wearing this necklace. According to folk tradition, if sailors saw dolphins by their boat after months at sea, they knew that they were near land. Sadly, my grandpa died last year, but I feel he's still with me. Dolphins are also a symbol of protection so my necklace not only protects me, but it also keeps me on the right track towards my next goal. I've got some important exams this year and I know my necklace is helping me stay focused on those. My grandpa would be very proud of me.

George, 18

If I hadn't visited Japan last year, I wouldn't have known what these were. These cute little cat figures were everywhere in shops and restaurants. In Japanese, they call them *Maneki-neko* which means 'beckoning cat'. Their origin dates back to the 17th century, the Edo period in Japan. Folk stories say that a rich man sheltered under a tree from a storm next to a temple. As luck would have it, he saw a cat waving to him and so he followed the cat into the temple. Suddenly, lightning struck the tree he had been under. If the man hadn't followed the cat, he would have died. The cat had saved his life. Today, the Maneki-neko cats wave their right and left paws. The left paw attracts customers to a business and the right paw invites good fortune. The cats come in different colours and each colour means something different. I bought a green one as a souvenir for my uncle. He was ill at the time and the green one brings good health. He got better very quickly. I bought a white one for myself, which sits on a shelf in my bedroom to bring me happiness and positive things in the future!

READING

1 Read the text quickly. Match the person with the charm they talk about.

1 Jody   a Dolphin
2 Aarya   b *Maneki-neko*
3 George   c Dreamcatcher

2 Read the text again and mark the sentences T (true), F (false) or DS (doesn't say).

1 Jody's dreamcatcher was a present. ☐
2 A dreamcatcher stops you having dreams. ☐
3 Aarya enjoys sailing. ☐
4 Aarya's necklace used to belong to her grandpa. ☐
5 George is from Japan. ☐
6 George's uncle is better now. ☐

3 CRITICAL THINKING **Read the statements. Which ones do you agree with? Why?**

1 'Lucky charms are a waste of time. It's just a way to make money, especially when they are sold as souvenirs.'
2 'I love my lucky charm. It makes me feel safe and I wouldn't go anywhere without it.'
3 'I create my own luck. I don't need any lucky charms to help me.'
4 'It's part of my culture and heritage. It's a big part of who I am. I'd never leave home without it.'

4 Write a short paragraph about a special charm from your country. Describe these things.

- its origins
- colours and materials
- why it is lucky

Writing a story about luck

1 INPUT **Read the story and put the pictures in order.**

A bit of luck

One day I took a bus into town on my own. I was really excited because I was wearing my new sunglasses for the first time. They're the best glasses ever. If I hadn't saved up for ages, I wouldn't have been able to buy them. To get to the point, I think it was money well spent.

I sat down, took the glasses off and looked at my phone. I chose my favourite playlist to listen to. I had my cool wireless earphones in and I couldn't have been happier. Well, to cut a long story short, when I got off the bus, I started to look for my glasses and … not there. My heart sank! I walked back towards the bus stop, but the bus had gone ages ago. Somehow, I'd left my brand new, expensive sunglasses on the bus!

I don't think I've ever felt so miserable in my life. I looked in some shop windows, but all I wanted to do was go home. I started walking but then, just as I was near a bus stop, I saw a bus coming, so I got on it. As I was paying the driver, I realised he looked familiar. Was it possible? Was this the same bus I'd used to go into town? I ran to the back, and there, on the floor under the seat – my sunglasses! I was speechless and over the moon. And I thought how lucky I was – if I hadn't seen the bus coming, I'd never have seen my sunglasses again.

2 ANALYSE **Read the story again. Answer the questions.**

1 In what two ways were the sunglasses important to the writer?

2 How did the writer feel when she discovered she didn't have her sunglasses?

3 When did she realise she might find her sunglasses again?

4 How did she feel when she found her sunglasses?

3 **Look at the story again. Find words or phrases which …**

1 are used to skip a part of the story.

_____

2 show how the writer felt at several different moments.

_____

4 PLAN **You are going to write a short story about 'a bit of luck'. It can be something that happened to you or to someone you know, or a made-up story.**

• What is the background to the story?

• What happened that was not good?

• What was the bit of luck that made things OK in the end?

5 PRODUCE **Write your story (250–300 words). Make sure you do the things below. Write your own checklist.**

• Think about the verb tenses you use.

• Use at least one mixed conditional sentence.

• Use adjectives and expressions showing how people felt at different moments in the story.

✔ CHECKLIST

☐ _____
☐ _____
☐ _____
☐ _____
☐ _____

 **LISTENING**

1 🔊 **3.02** **Read the sentences. Then listen and write the number of the conversation (1, 2 or 3).**

1 They are discussing how to replace something that was borrowed. ☐

2 They are discussing how to get somewhere without paying more than necessary. ☐

3 They are discussing the nature of quiz shows. ☐

2 🔊 **3.02** **Listen again and complete the sentences with three words.**

Conversation 1

1 Cheap train tickets to London
_____ after nine o'clock.

2 Julia thinks arriving in London at 9.55 is
_____ for her.

Conversation 2

3 Jakob likes the mixture of _____
in the quiz programme.

4 Sally prefers 'Mastermind' because contestants can _____ subject.

Conversation 3

5 Some of Pablo's stuff got _____
when he dropped his bag.

6 Pablo cannot replace the book because it costs
_____ pounds.

DIALOGUE

1 **Put the dialogue in the correct order.**

☐ Gina   Yes, and it didn't come for ages. And when it finally did come, it got stuck in a traffic jam, you know, it being rush hour at that time of day and all.

☐ Gina   Not wrong exactly – just not right! I was hoping I'd be back home in time for my favourite game show on TV, but the bus driver simply went past my stop without pulling over to pick me up! Just my luck.

[1] Gina   Today hasn't been my lucky day.

☐ Gina   No, and my mum didn't think to record it either. And I so badly wanted to see it.

☐ Martha   So you had to wait for the next one?

☐ Martha   Oh? Why's that? Did something go wrong?

☐ Martha   Bad luck. But don't worry, I'm sure they'll show it again before too long and we can record it for you.

☐ Martha   It's always bad after five o'clock, isn't it? But anyway, I'm guessing you didn't make it back home in time for the show?

PHRASES FOR FLUENCY SB p.36

1 **Complete the phrases with the missing letters.**

1 a _ _ _ m _ _ g

2 t _ _ t i _

3 a _ _ er a _ _

4 _ _ w a _ d _ _ain

5 W _ _ _ _ h _ _ _ _ you g _ _ to _ _ _ e?

6 We'll _ _ _ _ t s _ _ _ _ _ _ _ _ _ g o _ t.

2 **Complete the dialogues with phrases from Exercise 1.**

1 **A** I'm thinking about learning how to play chess. Do you think I'm mad?

   B Of course not. Go for it!
   _____

2 **A** What time does your cousin arrive tomorrow?

   B He'll be here at 11 o'clock,
   _____ the train's on time.

3 **A** Can I borrow your tablet?

   B Well, OK, provided you take really good care of it,
   _____ .

4 **A** You're listening to rap? I thought you were a rock fan!

   B Well, I am – but I don't mind a bit of rap
   _____ , just for a change.

5 **A** Hang on – how can we possibly go to the match and get back in time for the party tonight?

   B Yeah, it's tricky – but it's OK. _____ .

6 **A** You must be really pleased that you got 92 percent.

   B Yeah, kind of – but it was a really easy test,
   _____ .

C1 Advanced

EXAM GUIDE:

In Part 1 of the Listening exam, you hear three unrelated dialogues. Each one involves two speakers. The dialogues are taken from a wide range of contexts.

- Focus on the stem or question rather than the options when you listen. Choose the option that most closely matches what was said.
- The answers to the questions could come at any stage in the recording, so don't expect to hear things in the same order as in the questions.

1 🔊 3.03 **You will hear three different extracts. For questions 1–6, choose the answer (A, B or C) which fits best according to what you hear. There are two questions for each extract.**

Extract 1

You hear two geography students talking about a field trip they went on.

1 They agree that the trip was
  A too ambitious in what it tried to cover
  B so disorganised that it didn't keep to schedule
  C tiring because of the amount of walking involved

2 The male student feels that at the final stop on the trip, the tutor
  A wasn't as upset as the students assumed.
  B was justified in abandoning the visit.
  C was wrong to reveal his feelings.

Extract 2

You hear two friends talking about working from home.

3 What problem is the woman describing?
  A She loses concentration as the day progresses.
  B She finds it hard to get started on the most urgent tasks.
  C She keeps trying to deal with too many things at the same time.

4 How does she react to the idea of the 'proactive time' technique?
  A She's sceptical about whether it would suit her type of work.
  B She's concerned how it would impact on the rest of her commitments.
  C She's doubtful whether she'd have the necessary self-discipline to use it.

Extract 3

You hear two friends talking about wildlife photography.

5 When he was in Botswana, the man
  A experimented with different types of photographic equipment.
  B had guidance regarding the best photographic equipment to use.
  C kept his photographic equipment in a state of constant readiness.

6 In reply to the woman's question about setting up a shot, the man
  A admits that it's sometimes a matter of luck.
  B denies that it requires any particular level of skill.
  C explains that it's usually a long and complicated process.

→ SB p.40

Ⓖ GRAMMAR
Emphatic structures

1 ★★☆ **Complete the dialogue with *it's*, *what* or *all*. When there is a choice between *what* and *all*, think carefully about which word is best.**

Freya   I'm hungry. What shall we have for dinner?

Juan   Not much. ¹_____ there is in the fridge are four eggs.

Freya   Well, ²_____ you need to make an omelette is an egg and a frying pan. Can you make one?

Juan   Me? ³_____ always me who does the cooking.

Freya   That's because ⁴_____ me who is revising for final exams this week.

Juan   ⁵_____ I'd like to do is not cook a meal tonight.

Freya   I know what you mean. I'm quite tired. ⁶_____ I really want to do is stay in and watch TV.

Juan   Why don't we do something different tonight?

Freya   If you want me to cook, ⁷_____ you need to do is ask. I'd happily do it.

Juan   No, ⁸_____ I want is to get a takeaway and relax. We haven't done that for months. ⁹_____ doing something like that with my favourite housemate that I really miss.

Freya   OK, great idea! Let's have a look at some takeaway menus now.

2 ★★☆ **Rewrite the sentences using emphatic structures.**

0   He needs a good holiday.
What *he needs is a good holiday.*_____

1   I like a joke with a good punchline.
What _____

2   Jack's good at telling jokes, not his brother.
It's _____

3   You waste your time playing on your computer.
It's _____

4   She was only saying that you should take a break.
All _____

5   Olga only wants a sandwich for lunch.
All _____

3 ★★★ **Use cleft sentences to rewrite each pair of sentences. Use the underlined information as the focus. Use *it is / was* and *what* for each pair.**

0   a   <u>Leo</u> ate your sandwich.
     *It was Leo who ate your sandwich.*_____

   b   Leo ate your <u>sandwich</u>.
     *What Leo ate was your sandwich.*_____

1   a   You need to say '<u>sorry</u>'.
     _____

   b   <u>You</u> need to say 'sorry'.
     _____

2   a   My <u>dad</u> forgot the punchline.
     _____

   b   My dad forgot the <u>punchline</u>.
     _____

3   a   <u>I don't understand</u> why she said 'no'.
     _____

   b   I don't understand <u>why she said 'no'</u>.
     _____

4   a   I hate <u>cold showers</u> more than anything.
     _____

   b   I <u>hate</u> cold showers <u>more than anything</u>.
     _____

Boosting

→ SB p.43

4 ★☆☆ **Match two sentences with each picture.**

1 You've clearly never tried this before.
2 She's absolutely brilliant.
3 Well, it's undeniably the most unusual thing we've ever discovered.
4 She certainly knows how to entertain.
5 I've totally forgotten how to do this.
6 It's utterly delicious.
7 It's essentially half frog, half bird.
8 Well he definitely enjoyed that!

A   C

Cake Competition – judges

B   D

5 ★★☆ **Rewrite the sentences using the words in brackets.**

1 This is the best day of my life. (undeniably)
_____
2 I have made the best decision of my life. (certainly)
_____
3 I am the happiest man on the planet. (undoubtedly)
_____
4 It's what I've always wanted to do. (essentially)
_____
5 I can't wait to get started. (definitely)
_____
6 It is the job of my dreams. (literally)
_____
7 A chocolate taster! I mean, it's amazing. (utterly)
_____
8 And this company makes the best chocolates there are. (absolutely)
_____

6 ★★★ **Use the prompts to write sentences that are true for you.**

0 best day of my life / undeniably
The best day of my life was undeniably when I passed my driving test.

1 most interesting place in my town / undoubtedly
_____
2 most interesting school subject / certainly
_____
3 the best day of the week / clearly
_____
4 my favourite holiday destination / absolutely
_____
5 the best band in the world / unquestionably
_____
6 my favourite actor / definitely
_____

7 ★★★ **Add reasons to your sentences in Exercise 6.**

0 *It means that I can now go anywhere I like.*
_____

GET IT RIGHT!

Emphatic sentences

Learners at this level often use a subject pronoun instead of an object pronoun in cleft sentences beginning with *It's ...* . Another common error is using *it's ... what* instead of *it's ... that*.

✓ It's her who complains a lot. It's her attitude that really annoys me.
✗ It's ~~she~~ who complains a lot. It's her attitude ~~what~~ really annoys me.

Correct the errors in the sentences.

1 It's the release of endorphins what makes us feel good when we laugh.
_____
2 It's her sense of humour what I don't get.
_____
3 It's we who will have the last laugh when we win the tournament.
_____
4 It's he that is undoubtedly the best comedian in the country at the moment.
_____
5 It's they who will be laughing on the other side of their faces when their teacher finds out.
_____

VOCABULARY
Laughter

SB p.40

1 ⭐☆☆ **Match the sentence halves.**

1 Mr Thomas really has no sense of ☐
2 It's so embarrassing, but sometimes I get ☐
3 I've told you not to laugh ☐
4 I'm sorry, but I just don't find ☐
5 I like horror films that offer a little light ☐
6 He got right to the end of the joke and forgot ☐
7 That show was hilarious, ☐
8 I'm not really sure I got ☐

a it funny when you talk in that stupid voice.
b the punchline.
c I haven't laughed so much in a long time.
d relief at times to give you the chance to relax.
e at Tim. You know it upsets him.
f the giggles in the middle of Maths lessons.
g humour. In fact, I've never even seen him smile.
h the joke but I laughed anyway.

2 ⭐⭐⭐ **Complete the questionnaire. Then answer the questions.**

How good is your _____ of humour?

1 What do you do if you don't _____ a joke?
_____
_____

2 Everyone's laughing _____ you in a dream. How do you react?
_____
_____

3 You're telling a joke. It's going well. Disaster – you've forgotten the _____ ! What do you do?
_____
_____

4 It's the middle of an English lesson. You've got the _____ . Your teacher wants to know what it is you _____ so funny. What do you say?
_____
_____

Idioms with *laugh* and *joke*

SB p.43

3 ⭐⭐☆ **Complete the dialogues with *laugh(ed)*, *laughing*, *joke* or *joking*.**

1 A I'm thinking of entering your school's talent evening for parents.
  B Please don't, Dad. You'll be a _____ stock.
2 A Can you believe that Javi took his mum's car and he can't even drive?
  B It's no _____ matter, Liam. His parents found out and now he's in big trouble.
3 A Did you watch that new comedy series I told you about?
  B I certainly did. I _____ my head off.
4 A Have you heard about Don's new business idea? Isn't it ridiculous?
  B I know. I burst out _____ when I heard about it.
5 A Don't worry, Mum. I'll just eat oven chips every day.
  B _____ aside, Willem, do you really think you'll be able to look after yourself if you move out?
6 A £30 to order some flowers for my grandma's birthday and now the company wants to charge me another £10 for delivery.
  B I know. It's a _____ .
7 A The other team think it's funny that we're losing the match.
  B Don't worry, they'll be _____ on the other side of their faces when we score the winning goal.
8 A My friends all think it's funny that I didn't go to university.
  B Don't worry. You'll have the last _____ when you're running your own business by this time next year.

4 ⭐⭐⭐ **Complete the sentences with your own ideas.**

1 He might think it's funny to mess about in class, but he'll be laughing on the other side of his face when _____ .
2 I couldn't help myself. I just burst out laughing when _____ .
3 I can't believe _____ . It's a joke.
4 Don't _____ . You'll be a laughing stock.
5 Why are you giggling? It's no laughing matter when _____ .
6 I laugh my head off every time _____ .
7 I know you think it's silly that I want to swim across the Channel for charity, but joking aside, _____ .
8 So you didn't get a part in the school play? Well you'll have the last laugh when _____ .

REFERENCE

IDIOMS WITH *LAUGH* AND *JOKE*

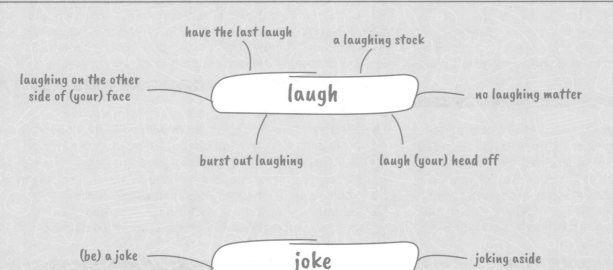

VOCABULARY EXTRA

1 Match the phrases in the list with the definitions. Use a dictionary if necessary.

> be doubled up | be in stitches
> chuckle | crack up | howl with laughter
> split your sides laughing

1 to laugh in a quiet way _____

2 to laugh heartily _____

3 to laugh out loud very hard _____

4 to laugh a lot at something _____

5 to bend over at the waist due to laughing _____

6 to laugh uncontrollably _____

2 Match the sentence halves.

1 Did you chuckle ☐

2 I was howling with ☐

3 We all cracked ☐

4 When was the last time you split ☐

5 The students doubled ☐

6 We were in ☐

a your sides laughing?

b stitches when we watched the comedy.

c laughter when I heard the punchline.

d up laughing when they heard the joke.

e when you found out the answer?

f up when we saw the video.

3 Answer the questions about you.

1 When was the last time you were in stitches? Why?

2 What makes you split your sides laughing?

3 Who do you know who always howls with laughter at jokes?

LAUGHTER 😂 THERAPY

Laughter not only provides a full-scale workout for your muscles, it unleashes a rush of stress-busting endorphins. What's more, your body can't distinguish between real and fake laughter – any giggle will do.

A ☐ The elation, or extreme happiness, you feel when you laugh is a great way of fighting the physical effects of stress. When we laugh, our body relaxes and endorphins (natural painkillers) are released into the blood stream.

A Laughter Therapist's aim is to help you laugh more easily. Therapy is available in group or individual sessions – these start with a warm-up followed by a range of activities designed to get you giggling. Laughter doesn't come easily to everyone, but luckily, it's a skill you can learn. So faking it has the same beneficial effect.

B ☐ Dr Lee Berk of Loma University Medical Centre, California, has been conducting laughter therapy research since the late 1970s. In 1989, Berk studied the effects of laughter in ten healthy males. Five experimental subjects watched an hour-long comedy while five control subjects didn't. Blood samples taken from the ten subjects revealed that cortisol (the hormone our body releases when under stress) in the experimental subjects had decreased more rapidly in comparison to the control group. Berk's research has also shown the number of cells that attack viruses and tumours increases through laughter. These same cells are blocked if the body suffers long-term stress.

C ☐ The therapeutic effects of laughter have been clinically studied since the 1970s, but Dr Madan Kataria – who developed laughter yoga in Mumbai – is credited with making laughter therapy more well known. Kataria set up the first laughter club in 1995. There are now more than 5,000 laughter clubs worldwide.

D ☐ Laughter therapy is suitable for everyone, although most therapists work within the healthcare profession or in the workplace, where laughter is used as a means of relieving stress.

Elderly groups, young people in care and mental health patients are all thought to benefit especially from laughter therapy. If you're undecided, remember this: children laugh about 400 times a day whereas adults manage a mere 15.

E ☐ A laughter therapy session may leave you feeling elated and exhausted in equal measure. Muscle tone and cardiovascular functions may be improved and oxygen levels in the blood may be boosted.

In the long term, laughter therapy teaches us that we don't just have to laugh when we are happy. Laughing in the face of anger, stress or anxiety – even if it's forced laughter – can actually lift your mood. And it's contagious, so you can expect to see those around you benefiting from a good giggle too.

📖 READING

1 **Read the article. What are the main benefits of laughter therapy?**

2 **Read the article again and match the headings (1–6) with the paragraphs (A–E). There is one extra heading.**

   1 Is there any evidence? ☐
   2 What is it? ☐
   3 Is it just a fad? ☐
   4 What results can I expect? ☐
   5 Where does it come from? ☐
   6 Who can do it? ☐

3 **CRITICAL THINKING** **Match the benefits of laughter (1–4) to the topics (a–d). Read the article to check. Can you add any more benefits?**

   1 Relieves stress and anxiety ☐
   2 Muscle tone and cardiovascular function improved; oxygen levels in the blood are boosted ☐
   3 Laughter is contagious; it makes other people feel better. ☐
   4 It makes you feel better and improves your state of mind. ☐

   a For other people
   b Mental health
   c Mood
   d Physical health

4 **What do you think about laughter therapy? Write a short paragraph explaining whether you think it would be good for you or not. Give reasons.**

DEVELOPING *Writing*

Writing a review

1 **INPUT** **Read the review. Which of the following does it NOT mention?**

☐ the characters   ☐ the plot
☐ the actors   ☐ the dialogue
☐ setting   ☐ the soundtrack

undeniably

It takes a special kind of series to survive a remake and that's what this 1990s series has done for this new season. As *Fuller House* embarks on this milestone, no one would be surprised if it went on for many more seasons. With the characters from the original series all grown up now, the show starts with flashbacks to the older show with the clever use of split screens.

In case you have never seen an episode, *Fuller House* is based on the 1990s series *Full House*. It follows the fortunes of recently widowed D.J. Tanner. She is a vet and is also the mother of three young boys. After the death of her husband she moves back into her childhood home with her father, Danny. But Danny has to move away for work while D.J. and the boys continue living in the house. D.J.'s sister, Stephanie, her best friend Kimmy and Kimmy's teenage daughter, Ramona, move in to help her and bring up the boys.

In terms of its concept as a family sitcom, *Fuller House* is nothing new. Neither is the grown-up child moving back into the parental home idea original. But then the show isn't really trying to redefine the genre. What *Fuller House* delivers so well are clever storylines, hilarious jokes – some from the original series – and, above all, well-rounded and lovable characters. One character in particular has helped transform the show into such a global hit. With her rebellious nature and under-achieving personality, Kimmy has become a firm favourite with fans.

I must admit that it took me a while to get into *Fuller House*, probably because I hadn't seen the original series. But I'm happy I stuck with it, because now I feel completely at home with this adorable cast of characters and the challenges they face living together under one roof. After all, learning about what's important in life and how much family and friends matter is what life is all about.

2 **ANALYSE** **Choose three of the boosting adverbs and decide where you could put them in the review. There are several possibilities.**

absolutely	certainly	clearly	definitely	entirely
essentially	literally	totally	~~undeniably~~
undoubtedly	unquestionably	utterly

3 **Read the review again and answer the questions.**

1 In paragraph 1, what factual information does the reviewer include in the introduction?
_____

2 In paragraph 2, why does the reviewer say 'In case …'?
_____

3 What is the purpose of this paragraph?
_____

4 In paragraph 3, what does the reviewer find unoriginal about the show?
_____

5 What does the reviewer like about the show?
_____

6 In paragraph 4, what relevance to our own lives does the writer feel the show has?
_____

4 **PLAN** **You are going to write a review of a TV or internet comedy series. Think about the questions in Exercise 3 for your series.**

5 **PRODUCE** **Write a review (220–260 words) of a TV or internet comedy series. Use your answers from Exercise 4 and the information in the tip box. Write your own checklist.**

✅ **CHECKLIST**

☐ _____
☐ _____

✏️ **WRITING TIP: REVIEWS**

- In your introduction, try to answer *wh-*questions. This will give your reader a good idea of what your subject is about. You might not be able to answer them all so choose the most relevant for your review.

- Don't give any spoilers (information that might ruin it for someone who hasn't seen it yet) and especially don't give away the ending. You might want to introduce a teaser, though. This information doesn't give anything away, but will make the reader interested to find out more.

- When you give your recommendations, be definitive – use extreme adjectives. Remember your job is to try to convince the reader one way or the other.

- Use cleft sentences to add greater emphasis.

🎧 LISTENING

1 🔊 **4.01** **Listen and write the answers to the jokes.**

1 **A** Knock, knock.
   B Who's there?
   A Harry.
   B Harry who?
   _____

2 Why did the students eat their homework?
   _____
   _____

3 What did the Science book say to the Maths book?
   _____

4 How do you make time fly?
   _____
   _____

2 🔊 **4.01** **Listen again and answer the questions.**

Conversation 1
1 Why doesn't Lidia find the joke funny?
   _____

2 What does Carl decide at the end?
   _____

Conversation 2
3 What do both dads agree is the best thing about having young children?
   _____

4 Where does Nat get all his jokes from?
   _____

Conversation 3
5 What does Suzi want help with?
   _____

6 How does Suzi feel about her mum's joke?
   _____

Conversation 4
7 What has Josh got a reputation for?
   _____

8 What does Ella suggest as a joke?
   _____

3 **Complete the lines from the conversations with the missing words.**

1 I heard what you said. I just
   _____ .

2 Ha ha, _____ . I'll have to tell that one to Nat. He'll love it.

3 That's _____ , Mum. Not! Now, can you help me, please?

4 That's so _____ –
   I _____ that one.

DIALOGUE

1 **Put the dialogue in order to make a joke.**

☐ **Teacher** OK, let me put it to you differently. If I gave you two apples, and another two apples and another two, how many would you have?

☐ **Teacher** No, listen carefully … If I gave you two cats, and another two cats and another two, how many would you have?

☒1 **Teacher** If I gave you two cats and another two cats and another two, how many would you have?

☐ **Teacher** Georgia, where on earth do you get seven from?

☐ **Teacher** Good. Now, if I gave you two cats, and another two cats and another two, how many would you have?

☐ **Georgia** I've already told you. I'd have seven.

☐ **Georgia** For the third time, I'd have seven.

☐ **Georgia** Because I've already got a cat!

☐ **Georgia** Six apples.

☐ **Georgia** Easy. I'd have seven cats.

2 **Write a short dialogue (8–10 lines) that includes a joke in it.**

_____
_____
_____
_____
_____
_____
_____
_____
_____

PRONUNCIATION
Telling jokes: pacing, pausing and punchlines
Go to page 119. 🎧

C1 Advanced

EXAM GUIDE:

In Part 3 of the Listening exam you will hear an interview or an exchange between two or more people.

- The rubric will give you some information about who and where these people are. This will help you prepare yourself for the kind of recording you will hear.
- In the exam paper there are six multiple-choice questions, each with four possible answers, from which you must choose the correct answer.
- You will have time before you listen so use this time wisely to carefully read though the questions. This will help prepare you for the content of the listening. It is also a good idea to underline the key points in the questions to help you focus better.
- You will need to listen out for attitude, opinion, agreement, gist, feeling, speaker purpose, function and detail.
- You will hear the recording twice, so use your second listening to confirm answers you already have and choose the best answers for those you didn't manage to get on the first listening.

1 🔊 **4.03** **You will hear an interview in which two comedians called Paula Owens and Dave Sharp are talking about their work. For questions 1–6, choose the answer (A, B, C or D) which fits best according to what you hear.**

1 Paula's first experience as a comedian came about as a result of
   A realising that she had some talent.
   B wanting to lend somebody her support.
   C being unable to resist a tempting challenge.
   D getting the chance to fulfill a long-held ambition.

2 Immediately after her first show, Paula felt
   A puzzled by the reaction of the audience.
   B annoyed at the weakness of the script.
   C relieved that it hadn't gone too badly.
   D guilty at having upset her partner.

3 What does Paula say about the manager of the first club where she worked?
   A She sometimes found his manner a bit too direct.
   B She's grateful that he gave her the space to develop.
   C She never found out why he decided to encourage her.
   D She's sorry that she didn't always meet his high standards.

4 What does Dave admit about his first solo comedy performance?
   A He underestimated how nervous he'd feel.
   B He should have prepared much more material.
   C It didn't go well because he was over-confident.
   D It required skills that didn't come naturally to him.

5 Dave and Paula agree that comedians
   A need to be ready to accept constructive criticism.
   B know how to get a hostile audience on their side.
   C find it hard to deal with the physical demands of the job.
   D are best ignoring provocative comments during their acts.

6 In contrast to Paula, Dave feels
   A concerned about his job security as a comedian.
   B that he still has new things to achieve as a comedian.
   C dissatisfied with some aspects of a comedian's lifestyle.
   D a need to develop new talents outside comedy as he gets older.

CONSOLIDATION

🎧 LISTENING

1 🔊 **4.04** **Listen and put the events in the order Rosie mentions them.**

Order of mention	Chronological order
☐ Rosie gets injured.	☐
☐ Rosie misses the school bus.	☐
☐ Rosie revises for her test.	☐
☐ Rosie's school bus breaks down.	☐
☐ Rosie's phone runs out of battery.	☐
☐ Rosie tries to have a hot bath.	☐
☐ Rosie finds out that the headteacher is teaching her class.	☐
☐ Rosie forgets her packed lunch.	☐
☐ Rosie is locked out of the house.	☐

2 🔊 **4.04** **Listen again and put the events above in chronological order.**

Ⓖ GRAMMAR

3 **Rewrite the sentences.**

1 John bought a new tablet. That's why he's got no money.
   If _____

2 If we don't leave now, we'll miss the train.
   Unless _____

3 The food was the only thing I liked about the party.
   All _____

4 I don't like seafood. That's why I didn't eat anything at the restaurant.
   If I _____

5 You have to invite Sasha to your party. Otherwise, she'll be really upset.
   If _____

6 I find waiting for hours in airports the most annoying thing about travelling.
   What _____

7 You really need to talk to Henry about the mess.
   It's _____

8 I'll tell you my secret as long as you promise not to tell anyone.
   Provided _____

ᴬᶻ VOCABULARY

4 **Complete the sentences with *laugh*, *joke* or *luck*.**

1 I win again. Better _____ next time.

2 They think you're crazy for training every day after school, but you'll have the last _____ when you get onto the national team.

3 It was a really good _____ , but I can't remember the punchline.

4 £10 is my final offer. It's a good price, so don't push your _____ .

5 Maybe I didn't get it, but I didn't think that _____ was very funny.

6 It's raining and my umbrella's at home. That's just my _____ .

7 Change for a £10 note? Let me see. You're in _____ . Here you are.

8 £5 for a can of cola. That's a _____ , right?

5 **Match the sentence halves.**

1 Can you believe it? It turned ☐
2 Careful you don't fall ☐
3 This is the fifth time we've been ☐
4 That's great news! I'm really happy things have worked ☐
5 I felt bad, but I couldn't help but burst ☐
6 If you're bored all the time, why don't you take ☐
7 It's not kind to laugh ☐
8 This is so hard and the weather is getting worse. Let's turn ☐

a up a new hobby to fill up your time?
b over the dog when you leave.
c back now while we can.
d at him when he's learning to drive.
e out Kris was in my class at nursery school!
f out laughing when Dad walked into the door.
g over this and you still don't understand.
h out for you and Carly.

DIALOGUE

6 Put the dialogue in order.

☐	Robin	Ha ha! Very funny.
☐	Robin	Of course it does, assuming you believe in these things, that is.
☐	Robin	Don't mention it. Let's call it £5.
☐	Robin	Well, if I didn't have this coin, I certainly wouldn't have passed the mid-term exams.
1	Robin	Have I shown you my lucky pound coin?
☐	Robin	No, I'm serious. It's a bargain. It really works. What have you got to lose?
☐	Robin	Well you can have this one, if you want.
☐	Jenni	Only £4!
☐	Jenni	I do. I really do. So how has it helped you?
☐	Jenni	£5! Ha! That's a good one, Robin.
☐	Jenni	Really? I could do with something like that.
☐	Jenni	No you haven't, does it work?
☐	Jenni	Wow! Thanks. That's really kind of you.

READING

7 Read the article and answer the questions.

1 Why was the Laugh Lab set up?

_____
_____
_____

2 What were visitors to the Laugh Lab's site asked to do?

_____
_____
_____

3 What differences did they find in the European sense of humour and the English-speaking world's sense of humour?

_____
_____
_____

4 What rather unusual facts did the survey discover?

_____
_____
_____

✏ WRITING

8 What is your favourite joke? Translate it into English and write it down. Does it still sound funny?

 THE LAUGH LAB

was an ambitious online scientific investigation into the nature of humour in an attempt to find out what makes us laugh and why. Among other things, it set out to discover the world's funniest joke, whether there was a difference in what men and women found funny, how age affects our sense of humour and how different nationalities respond to different types of jokes.

For one year, the Laugh Lab's online site was visited by thousands of people from all over the world. They were asked to submit their favourite joke before going on to answer questions about themselves such as their age, sex and nationality. They were also asked to rate a number of jokes sent in by others using a specially designed 'giggleometer'. From a database of over 40,000 jokes and 1.5 million ratings, the researchers were able to draw some pretty definitive conclusions. For example …

The Germans were found to have the best sense of humour and laughed readily at a variety of different types of joke. They were followed by the French and the Danish. English-speaking countries such as the UK, the US, New Zealand and Australia tended to enjoy jokes which involved word play such as:

> **Patient** Doctor, doctor. I keep thinking I'm a bridge.
> **Doctor** What's come over you?
> **Patient** Two cars, a lorry and a motorbike.

Many Europeans, on the other hand, tended to go for more surrealist jokes such as:

> A dog went to a telegram office, took out a blank form and wrote: 'Woof. Woof. Woof. Woof. Woof. Woof. Woof. Woof. Woof.'
> The clerk examined the paper and politely told the dog: 'There are only nine words here. You could send another 'Woof' for the same price.' 'But,' the dog replied, 'that would make no sense at all.'

The survey also came up with a number of more bizarre findings. For example, it discovered that the time of day and the day of the month also had an effect on how funny a joke was found to be. It determined that the ideal time to tell a joke was 6.03 pm on the 15th day of any month. It also found that the perfect length for a joke was 103 words and that the funniest animal in jokes was the duck.

5 WHAT A THRILL!

Grammar video

GRAMMAR
Participle clauses

→ SB p.50

1 ⭐☆☆ **Read the email about a day out at Cheddar Gorge in England. Five of the participles in italics need to be changed to a past participle. Circle the mistakes and then correct them.**

¹*Feeling* adventurous, my friend and I booked a day of climbing and caving at Cheddar Gorge. ²*Not being* an experienced climber, I felt a bit nervous about the day. ³*Not liking being* in small spaces, my friend was also nervous. ⁴*Advising* by a friend, we chose to go with a company called Rocksport. That morning, ⁵*dressing* in overalls, boots and hats we headed for the caves with our instructor. ⁶*Seeing* the ladders descending down into the darkness, the adrenalin kicked in. ⁷*Crawling* through small gaps in the rock was sometimes scary, but overall, I enjoyed the experience. After lunch we went climbing. ⁸*Encouraging* by the instructor, we cautiously ascended the rock face. ⁹*Warning* by a friend, I didn't look down – not even once. On finally ¹⁰*reaching* the top, I felt an overwhelming sense of achievement. Then ¹¹*abseiling* back down was great fun. ¹²*Filming* by a friend on the ground, I have a lovely record of that memorable afternoon.

2 ⭐⭐☆ **Circle the correct past or present participle to complete the sentences.**

1 *Motivating / Motivated* by the video, I decided to try zip-wiring.

2 *Paragliding / Paraglided* towards the beach, I felt the biggest thrill of my life.

3 *Going / Gone* into the cave, I felt my heart beat faster and faster.

4 *Inspiring / Inspired* by my mother, I decided to climb Mount Everest.

5 *Training / Trained* by an expert, he was ready to do the jump.

6 *Watching / Watched* my sister abseil down the side of the building, I started to get really nervous.

7 *Climbing / Climbed* back down the cliff, I had to concentrate on not looking down.

8 *Surrounding / Surrounded* by mountains, the place was perfect for a climbing school.

3 ⭐⭐☆ **Complete the text with the correct form of the verbs.**

While ¹_____ (climb) a cliff face in Cornwall, Max Kidman's safety rope broke. ²_____ (fall) 30 metres, he luckily landed on some grass which saved his life. However, ³_____ (break) his leg, he was unable to climb down to the beach. ⁴_____ (watch) by his family and friends, he was rescued by helicopter. Then, ⁵_____ (take) to hospital by the helicopter, he felt lucky to be alive. ⁶_____ (phone) the emergency services had saved his life. Later, when ⁷_____ (interview) by a reporter from a local newspaper, he gave an account of the events. '⁸_____ (have) this accident won't stop me from climbing again,' he said.

4 ⭐⭐☆ **Rewrite the sentences using a perfect participle.**

0 'I've paraglided before. I'm not scared,' she said.
   Having paraglided before, she wasn't scared.

1 'I've watched the video lots of times, so I know what happens,' he said.
   _____

2 'I've been scuba diving and now I'd like to try deep sea diving,' she said.
   _____

3 'I enjoyed caving in Wales, I want to do it again,' he said.
   _____

4 'I've worked as a stunt person in films, so I'm used to performing dangerous stunts,' she said.
   _____

5 'I've never been keen on heights so I don't think I can do a bungee jump,' he said.
   _____

5 ★★☆ **Rewrite the sentences by turning the underlined part of the sentence into a participle clause.**

1 <u>I trained for six months.</u> I was ready to run the marathon.

_____

2 <u>I watched the video.</u> It reminded me of the parachute jump.

_____

3 <u>She climbed Mount Kilimanjaro.</u> She was ready to climb Mount Everest.

_____

4 <u>He was afraid of heights.</u> He couldn't look down.

_____

5 <u>He was trained by an Olympic athlete.</u> He was fit enough to trek across the desert.

_____

6 <u>She had done a bungee jump before.</u> She wasn't worried.

_____

6 ★★☆ **Use the prompts to write sentences. Use a present participle and *after*, *before*, *since*, *while* or *on*. More than one answer is possible.**

0 ski / on holiday / I / break / my leg
  While skiing on holiday, I broke my leg.

1 practise / on / an indoor climbing wall / I / ready / to climb / outdoors

_____

2 sign up for / a parachute jump / he / not able to sleep

_____

3 learn / his daughter / win / the marathon / he / be / very proud

_____

4 break / his leg / he / not do / any more climbing

_____

5 do / her first parachute jump / she / do / three practice jumps

_____

6 watch / a film / set in the Alps / she / decide / join / a climbing club

_____

7 see / his friend / be afraid / he / climb back up / to help / him

_____

Verbs of perception with infinitive or gerund

 SB p.53

7 ★★☆ **Complete the sentences with the correct form of the verbs in the list.**

> beat | blow | fall | grip | laugh | shine

1 He felt a hot wind _____ across his face. Then he started to walk across the desert.

2 We could hear people _____ so we knew they were enjoying the show.

3 If you look out of the window now, you can still see the sun _____ on the walls of the castle.

4 I was scared. I could feel my heart _____ very fast.

5 We could hear raindrops _____ on the rooftop.

6 I felt his hand _____ my arm as he tried to stop me. I pulled my arm away and I carried on running.

GET IT *RIGHT!*

Participle clauses

Learners often make mistakes with participle clauses. When wanting to indicate that one activity happened after another, *having* + past participle is necessary. If the activities happened at the same time, a present participle is required.

✓ *Having finished his project, James then went home.*

✗ ~~Finishing~~ *his project, James then went home.*

Rewrite the sentences using a participle clause. Change the verbs in bold to become the participle.

0 The stunt person **leapt** from the top of the building. Then she landed on some mattresses below.

  Having leapt from the top of the building, the stunt person landed on some mattresses below.

1 The risks **were minimised**, so the film director decided to go ahead with the stunt.

_____

2 The teacher **made** his point loud and clear and told the students that they wouldn't pass the exam unless they revised.

_____

3 They **painted** Megan's bedroom and then bought new furniture for it.

_____

4 She **agreed** with us initially, but then told us that she wouldn't do it.

_____

5 Dan's mother **heard** him sing and felt very proud.

_____

6 Saul **did** one bungee jump and now can't wait to do another!

_____

VOCABULARY
Thrill seeking

→ SB p.51

1 ★☆☆ **Match the words to make phrases.**

1 death-	☐	**a**	the risk
2 dare	☐	**b**	out of
3 minimise	☐	**c**	devil
4 get a kick	☐	**d**	taker
5 risk-	☐	**e**	defying

2 ★★☆ **Circle the correct words.**

1 That was an amazing *stunt / daredevil*! I didn't think he could cycle along that wall.
2 Alice isn't a *risk-taker / stunt*. She doesn't do anything unless she knows it's safe.
3 He performed one more *risk-taker / death-defying* stunt on his motorbike.
4 Sarah *gets a kick out of / assesses* the risk of base jumping. She really loves it.
5 The safety harness *assesses / minimises* the risk of having an accident.
6 He is successful because he is *minimising the risks / audacious* and not afraid to take risks.
7 The instructor *assessed the risk / got a kick out of it* before we began the climb.
8 Matt's a complete *audacious / daredevil*. He's not scared of anything.

3 ★★☆ **Complete the dialogue with the words/ phrases in the list.**

> assess the risk | audacious | daredevil
> death-defying | get a kick out of | stunt

Anna Will you come and do a bungee jump with me?

Joel You're kidding. I can't think of anything worse.

Anna Oh go on. You always ¹_____ rollercoasters. And what about that amazing ²_____ on the skateboard you did on Saturday? That was a real ³_____ move.

Joel Yeah, but a bungee jump's different. I'm not afraid of heights, but I don't think I could do a bungee jump or go base jumping.

Anna Come on, Joel. You're a ⁴_____ . You love taking risks. You're an ⁵_____ climber.

Joel Yes, I take risks. But I always ⁶_____ before I do a skateboard stunt or climb a cliff face.

4 ★★★ **Choose two of these questions to write about.**

1 Describe the best stunt you've seen in a film.
2 What do you get a kick out of? Why?
3 Think of a dangerous activity. What are the risks involved and how can you minimise them?
4 Which of your friends is the biggest daredevil? What sort of things do they do?

Idioms with *hot* and *cold*

→ SB p.53

5 ★★☆ **Complete the dialogues with *hot* or *cold* idioms.**

1 **A** What's up, Alfie? You look a bit stressed.
   B I'm _____ again with my mum and dad. I got home really late last night.

2 **A** Why don't we do a bungee jump this weekend?
   B I don't want to _____ that idea, but Katie's afraid of heights.

3 **A** Why are you upset, Noah?
   B Sophie gave me _____ again at the party last night. She didn't talk to me at all.
   A Don't get all _____ about it. I'm sure you'll sort it out with her.

4 **A** I think we should go over and talk to Isaac.
   B You're right. We shouldn't _____ him out _____ any more, even if we don't agree with what he said.

5 **A** Wow! You look all _____ . What's wrong?
   B I forgot that I've got an exam in five minutes!

6 ★★★ **Choose four of the idioms and write your own short dialogues.**

1 A _____
     _____
  B _____
     _____

2 A _____
     _____
  B _____
     _____

3 A _____
     _____
  B _____
     _____

4 A _____
     _____
  B _____
     _____

REFERENCE
Thrill seeking

nouns	adjectives	verbs
stunt	audacious	assess the risk
daredevil	death-defying	minimise the risk
risk-taker		get a (real) kick out of

hot under the collar

give somebody the cold shoulder

hot and bothered

Idioms with hot and cold

be in hot water

leave somebody out in the cold

pour cold water on something

VOCABULARY EXTRA

1 Complete the definitions with the words in the list.

> risk life and limb | scared out of your wits | scared stiff
> take your life in your hands | your heart misses a beat

1 _____ extremely frightened
2 _____ do something that is very dangerous, especially when you risk death
3 _____ you feel very excited or nervous
4 _____ feel so afraid or scared, it makes you panic
5 _____ do something very dangerous that could cause a serious injury or even death

2 Complete the idioms in the dialogues.

1 A What about being a firefighter?
   B No, thanks. I don't want to _____ every day to save people.
2 A When you were young, you were scared _____ of speaking in front of the class.
   B I know and now I'm an actor! My heart still _____ before I go on stage, though.
3 A It's so dark and so quiet. What's that strange noise?
   B I don't know. I'm scared _____ . Run!
4 A You take _____ trying to cross the road in this part of the city.
   B I know, there's always so much traffic.

3 Complete the sentences so they are true for you.

1 I was scared out of my wits when … _____
2 I felt I took my life in my hands when … _____
3 My heart always misses a beat when … _____

PRONUNCIATION
Connected speech feature: elision
Go to page 119.

Thrillseekers

Feel the fear!

On 21 April, 2009, the extreme kayaker Tyler Bradt kayaked over Washington's 57-metre high Palouse Falls. He plunged over the waterfall in his canoe and survived the death-defying free-fall with just a broken paddle and a sprained wrist. We can't all be Tyler Bradt, but we can all be risk-takers in our own way. Here are just a few thrill-seeking adventures for all you daredevils out there to read about and imagine the adrenaline rush. Read on and feel the fear.

Zhangjiajie Glass Bridge, China
Fear factor: ★★★★★

There's a new way to enjoy the incredible views here – a 100-metre-long glass skywalk. It's the third of its kind in this area. It doesn't require any climbing skills. It just requires you to be a thrill-seeker with a love of fear.

The quickest and easiest way to reach the skywalk is to take a cable car to the mountain top. It takes about half an hour. After that, you will need to walk for another 400 metres to reach the skywalk. At this point, you will be more than 1400 metres above the ground.

Once you get to the skywalk, you can see all the way down to the bottom of the cliff and the road up the mountain. The skywalk stretches 100 metres around the mountain and is 1.6 metres wide.

Some people find it difficult to enjoy the breathtaking views and spine-tingling thrill of looking down once they are there because they are so terrified. It's a great place for an extreme selfie, but it is definitely not for the faint-hearted.

Stratosphere SkyJump – Las Vegas, US
Fear factor: ★★★★

You can push your fear of heights to the limit on the 108th floor of the STRAT Hotel in Las Vegas. With breathtaking views over the city below, the SkyJump is a once-in-a-lifetime experience. Where else can you see the Las Vegas Strip from a height of 253 metres and nothing but sky between you and the ground? Your SkyJump starts once you exit the lift. Then you have to put on your harness and after safety checks are completed, it's over to you. The best way to take the plunge is to count to three and jump. It's guaranteed to make your heart beat very fast and take your breath away – literally!

Thorpe Park, England
Fear factor: ★★★

Thorpe Park in Surrey, England, is one of the most popular amusement parks for thrill-seekers and daredevils. Try Colossus, the world's first rollercoaster with ten inversions! It has a maximum speed of 72 kilometres per hour, with a drop of 30 metres, and a maximum height of 30 metres. It has so many twists and turns over 850 metres that it will make your head spin!

If that's not thrilling enough, you could try the Stealth ride which combines speed and height to create the ultimate thrill ride. At 62.5 metres high and a maximum speed of 80 kilometres per hour, it reaches its maximum speed in less than two seconds. It's one of the biggest adrenaline rushes you'll ever feel. If you get a kick out of going on rollercoasters, then Thorpe Park is the place for you.

READING

1 Look at the online guide. What one thing do you need to try the activities in the photos?

    A a love of fear   **C** immense skill

    B a love of heights   **D** climbing technique

2 Read the online guide and complete the sentences with between one and three words.

    1 Tyler Bradt _____ Washington's Palouse Falls and survived.

    2 The Zhangjiajie Glass Bridge is the third _____ in this area of China.

    3 There is a drop of _____ below the skywalk.

    4 The Stratosphere SkyJump starts on the _____ of the STRAT Hotel.

    5 To do the Stratosphere SkyJump, you must _____ .

    6 Thorpe Park is great if you enjoy _____ .

3 **CRITICAL THINKING** Look at this list of activities. Rate the fear factor in these activities for you (5 = most frightening). Then explain the reasons for your choices.

- a ride on Colossus ☐
- diving with sharks ☐
- the Stratosphere SkyJump ☐
- a bungee jump ☐
- the Glass Bridge in Zhangjiajie ☐
- a hot-air balloon ride ☐

4 Write a short paragraph about a time you faced your fears. How did you feel before, during and after the event? Describe your feelings.

DEVELOPING *Writing*

Writing an article

1 **INPUT** **Read Nina's article for the school magazine and answer the questions.**

1 What is the article about?
2 What did Nina do and why?
3 How does she describe her feelings at different stages?
4 How was the experience?

A thrill to remember

¹*Motivated / Motivating* by my love of the outdoors, I volunteered to snowboard down a mountain to raise money for a local hospital. I had never snowboarded in my life before, so I had a lot of work to do.

After ²*practising / practised* for several weeks indoors with an instructor, the day finally arrived for me to snowboard down a real mountain in the snow. My instructor was going to snowboard down with me that day. So, ³*being given / having been given* my snowboard, I put on my boots, goggles and helmet. Then after ⁴*putting / put* my feet onto the board, I was ready to for my first solo descent of a mountain. ⁵*Having known / Knowing* that I was now standing on my snowboard and that there was an instructor beside made me feel more confident. ⁶*Feeling / Felt* only slightly nervous, I stood at the top and waited with the other snowboarders. However, as I waited for my turn to start, **A** ☐. I was scared.

Finally, the moment came. I stood and looked down at the white mountain below me and I started to move. I was moving slowly at first and then suddenly very fast. Down and down I went and **B** ☐. I realised I was doing it – I was actually snowboarding! ⁷*Having relaxing / Having relaxed*, I started to enjoy the feeling of moving smoothly down the mountain. As I got closer to the bottom, **C** ☐. After ⁸*stopping / stopped* suddenly with a thud in the thick snow, I felt a huge sense of relief. My friends, ⁹*watched / watching* from the bottom, ran to congratulate me.

¹⁰*Experienced / Having experienced* the thrill of snowboarding once, I can't wait to do it again. We raised £1,000 that day and I had one of the greatest experiences of my life.

2 **ANALYSE** **Read the article again. Circle the correct participles.**

3 **Complete the article with the missing information (1–3).**

1 I heard cheering and clapping
2 I felt my legs shaking and my heart beating very fast
3 I could feel the wind whistling in my ears

4 **Read the article again and answer the questions.**

1 What special equipment did she need?
_____
2 What made her feel more confident about snowboarding?
_____
3 When did she feel very nervous?
_____
4 Who was waiting for her at the bottom?
_____
5 How did she describe the day?
_____

✎ WRITING TIP: AN ARTICLE

- Remember to answer all the *wh-* questions before you start your article.
- Use participle clauses to allow you to describe situations in a more concise way.
- Use verbs of perception to make your article more interesting.

5 **PLAN** **Think about a thrilling experience you have had or would like to have. Use the questions in Exercise 4 to help you write about your experience.**

6 **PRODUCE** **Write an article (200–250 words) for your school magazine about a thrilling experience. Use your ideas from Exercise 5 and the Writing tip. Write your own checklist.**

✔ CHECKLIST

☐ _____
☐ _____
☐ _____
☐ _____
☐ _____

🎧 LISTENING

1 🔊 5.02 **Listen to the conversation. What do these numbers refer to?**

a 63

b 45

c 100

2 🔊 5.02 **Listen again and answer the questions.**

1 What extraordinary thing have Will Gadd and Sarah Hueniken done?

_____

2 What have 15 other people done?

_____

3 What is Jane's opinion of Will and Sarah?

_____

4 What does Tony think about people who would do something like the climb?

_____

5 How long did the climb take Will and Sarah?

_____

6 What does Tony think is the best thing about the climb?

_____

3 🔊 5.02 **Listen again and complete these parts of the dialogue.**

1

Jane She survived but she did say that no one should do that ever again.

Tony _____ . You'd be mad to throw yourself over a waterfall in a barrel.

Jane _____ , you've got to live a bit dangerously.

2

Jane They've climbed a 45-metre-high frozen waterfall.

Tony _____ . That's a pretty cool achievement.

Jane To come up with an idea like that, then to plan it and organise it, then to actually do it ... that's awesome.

Tony _____ . However, I still think you have to be a little crazy to do something like that.

Jane _____ . I think they're incredibly brave.

3

Jane I'm surprised they got permission from the authorities in the first place.

Tony _____ . How long did it take to get permission?

Jane It took them a year.

Tony _____ , the best thing about it is getting to see these beautiful photographs of the ice falls.

Jane _____ . It's great that we get to share the view with Will and Sarah.

DIALOGUE

1 **Put the words in order to complete the dialogues.**

1

Maria Hi, Sofia. How did your audition go yesterday?

it / hear / about / all / wait / can't / to / I

_____ .

Sofia I don't think I'll get a part in the school play.

Maria come? / actress / brilliant / You're / a / How

_____ .

Sofia I couldn't remember my lines. It was awful.

2

Jake Are you going to help me with the washing up, Grace?

Grace No. I'm busy.

Jake But you never do anything around the house.

Grace no, / here / go / we / Oh

_____ .

Jake You're always on your phone or on your laptop.

potato / into / a / couch / You're / turning

_____ .

3

Will Why are you so tired, Joe?

Joe I'm not sure.

go / did / I / sleep / to / late / really / last / night

_____ .

I started browsing the internet and I couldn't stop.

Will That explains it, then.

Joe What?

Will mean / I / know / You / what

_____ .

You need to get some sleep. You should leave your phone in the living room at night. Problem solved.

2 **Choose a situation. Write a dialogue (8–10 lines). First, disagree with your friend, then accept your friend's point.**

- Your friend says that it's your fault that the team you were playing in lost the football/ tennis match on Saturday. You disagree.

- Your friend says you got too many answers wrong in the quiz, so your team lost. You disagree.

C1 Advanced

1 **You are going to read an article about a motorcycle sport. For questions 1–6, choose the answer (A, B, C or D) which you think fits best according to the text.**

MOTORCYCLE PARENTING

When speaking to my son Cosmo, I try to avoid sentences that begin with the words: 'When I was your age …' on the basis that it eliminates the need for him to roll his eyes. So it was gratifying to discover that not only is he enjoying a particular long-held passion of mine, but that he was drawn to it as a result of his own genuine curiosity rather than my prompting. Entirely of his own volition, he's recently become hooked on trials riding, a once-niche form of off-road motorcycling that's now enjoying a cult following amongst extreme-sports fans.

My own obsession with it began at the age of 13 – exactly my son's age now. My hero was a middle-aged, slightly chubby individual called Don Smith. He had jet-black hair and mainly rode in jeans, a waxed jacket and a fisherman's sweater as he raced bikes up rock-strewn streams, through muddy ruts and over the fallen trunks of giant trees on his way to major victories at home and abroad. As many champions do, he retired and wrote a book. It was called *Ride It! The Complete Book of Motorcycle Trials*, I first became aware of it when I happened to spot a copy in the window of a motor accessories shop as I was cycling home from school. It was by no means cheap, and I spent many an anxious

moment worrying that it would be snapped up by another trials fan before I could raise the funds to acquire it. But I guess no such kindred spirit existed in my part of town, however, because after many weeks of saving I was able to secure the display copy of the book, which emerged from the window draped in cobwebs with its cover faded by the sun.

Despite having neither a bike nor anywhere to ride one, I proceeded to study and absorb all the book's contents with an intensity that my teachers wouldn't have believed me capable of. I read and re-read each chapter, marvelling at the black-and-white images of Smith practising on his Kawasaki KT250, as he hopped over the top of a Coca-Cola can without touching it with either wheel – and then doing the same thing with a 40-gallon oil drum laid on its side. My son's trials-riding heroes are from quite a different stable. They have *line 47* cool names such as Adam Raga and Toni Bou and wear brightly coloured outfits that follow every contour of their finely honed bodies; their *line 50* bikes and kit emblazoned with sponsorship logos; they're almost invariably light-hearted *line 52* and, when off-duty, they post Instagram shots of themselves lounging on the beach. *line 54*

1 In the first paragraph, the writer expresses feelings of
  A pride in his son's success in competitions.
  B surprise at his son's sudden change of attitude.
  C relief that his son has now started to follow his advice.
  D pleasure in finding he has a common interest with his son.

2 What do we discover about Don Smith's book in the second paragraph?
  A The writer had been looking for it for some time.
  B It was only available from very specialist retailers.
  C It wasn't as popular as the writer thought it might be.
  D The price reflected how difficult it was to find a copy.

3 In the third paragraph, the writer reveals that he
  A tried to copy some of Don Smith's tricks on his own bike.
  B wasn't the sort of teenager who generally spent time reading.
  C now realises that Don Smith wasn't such an impressive rider.
  D was more interested in the book's illustrations that than the text.

4 Which of the following phrases used to describe Cosmo's heroes contrasts directly with the writer's description of Don Smith in the second paragraph?
  A quite a different stable (line 47)
  B finely honed bodies (line 50)
  C invariably light-hearted (line 52)
  D lounging on the beach (line 54)

6 FAMOUS LIVES

Grammar video
▶15

→ SB p.58

@ GRAMMAR

Modals 1: *may, might, can, could, will, won't*

1 ⭐☆☆ **Decide if the underlined part of each sentence refers to the past (P), general time (GT) or the future (F).**

1 We might be right to say no to nuclear weapons but I hope we won't be proved wrong. ☐

2 The cold weather may be the result of strong sea currents from the south. ☐

3 We won't know his answer until next week. ☐

4 I will give you a call when I arrive. ☐

5 Don't tell her too much. She could be a spy. ☐

6 I could see she was upset and I wanted to know if I could help. ☐

7 Dad won't give me any money, so I can't go to the concert. ☐

8 Bears are very protective of their young and they will do anything to keep them safe. ☐

9 Following a football team can be quite hard at times. ☐

10 Fans must have been disappointed when she cancelled her show. ☐

2 ⭐⭐☆ **Cross out the option in each sentence that is NOT possible.**

1 You *might / could / will* be forgiven for thinking he doesn't care but he's just really busy.

2 The strange lights that have been seen in the sky *might / may / can* just be airplanes.

3 The influence of Picasso on his work *might / can / could* be seen in his later paintings.

4 The fact she's not answering her phone *may / won't / could* mean that she hasn't heard it.

5 Dogs *will / can / could* act more aggressively when they are together.

6 My dad just *won't / doesn't / might not* listen to anything I say.

7 Their latest single *can / may / might* just be their best.

8 We *couldn't / mightn't / didn't* understand a word that he said.

3 ⭐⭐☆ **Complete each pair of sentences with the same modal verb: *might, can, could, will* or *won't*.**

1 a Paul _____ return my phone calls. Have I done something to upset him?

   b I _____ be home before 8 o'clock, so don't wait for me to eat.

2 a Sitting exams _____ be a very stressful time for some students.

   b Have you seen him play? He _____ do incredible things with a guitar.

3 a It _____ be many years before scientists finally find a cure for the disease.

   b I _____ name every capital city in the world when I was eight, but I've forgotten most of them.

4 a Miss Dawes _____ always help you if she can.

   b I believe that it _____ soon be normal to live to 150.

5 a You _____ think she's a bit rude, but the truth is she's very shy.

   b Owen _____ know the answer, he's pretty good at these things.

4 ⭐⭐⭐ **Complete the sentences with your own ideas.**

1 It's no good. He just won't
_____ .

3 Be careful. It might
_____ .

2 It's not a bad job but it can
_____ .

4 I'm not sure this film will
_____ .

Modals 2: *should, shouldn't, must, mustn't, can't*

→ SB p.61

5 ★☆☆ **Match the sentences.**

1 He must know a lot of people. ☐
2 You must study harder. ☐
3 She shouldn't listen to such loud music. ☐
4 You shouldn't worry about me. ☐
5 You can't go in there. ☐
6 He can't be 50. ☐
7 You mustn't eat the tomatoes. ☐
8 You mustn't get so nervous. ☐
9 You should give him a call. ☐
10 You should get on the train. ☐

a I'll be fine.
b He looks too young.
c I need them for dinner tonight.
d It'll spoil your performance.
e He'll be worried about you.
f I've never been to such a busy party.
g It's ready to leave.
h You're going to do badly in the exams if you don't.
i It's private property.
j She'll have problems with her hearing.

6 ★★☆ **Match each sentence with its function. Mark the sentences E (expectation), S (strong advice), R (reasonableness) or A (advice).**

0 She must be happy that she got the job. [E]
1 You must wear a hat today. ☐
2 It should be a nice day tomorrow. ☐
3 He can't be a professional singer. ☐
4 You should get a good night's sleep. ☐
5 We should have enough food for the picnic. ☐
6 You mustn't say a word. ☐
7 They mustn't get too worried. ☐
8 He shouldn't eat so much. ☐
9 You shouldn't expect him to answer your email immediately. ☐

7 ★★★ **Write a follow-on for each of the sentences in Exercise 6.**

0 *She's always wanted to work in fashion.*
1 _____
2 _____
3 _____
4 _____
5 _____
6 _____
7 _____
8 _____
9 _____

GET IT RIGHT!

Modals

Learners often confuse the different modals: *should, shouldn't, must, mustn't, can't, won't, would.*

✓ I don't think you should do that – it's wrong.
✗ I don't think you ~~must~~ do that – it's wrong.
✓ Ben won't come unless you ask him.
✗ Ben ~~mustn't~~ come unless you ask him.

Rewrite the sentences with the correct modal verb.

1 Do you think you would do that for me? I'd be very grateful.

_____

2 That actress mustn't be invited on the chat show, surely? She's not an A-list celebrity!

_____

3 He should definitely try and keep a low profile if it meant he could keep the paparazzi away.

_____

4 I can't imagine that any celebrity should ever wish to disappear without a trace.

_____

5 Julia is totally fixated on that band. Perhaps she would see a doctor. It's not healthy.

_____

6 If Simon wants to keep his friends, he couldn't keep boring them with details of his celebrity obsession.

_____

PRONUNCIATION
Modal stress and meaning Go to page 119. 🎧

VOCABULARY
Admiration

1 ★★☆ **Complete the sentences with the correct form of the words and phrases in the list.**

> addicted | centre of attention
> fascination with | fixated | huge fan
> idol | obsession | worship

1 They're _____ on having a career in music. I'm not sure they're good enough.

2 I think you might have an unhealthy _____ with that singer. Do you agree?

3 I think I might be _____ to social media. I check my phone all the time.

4 My younger brother has a _____ how things work. He loves taking old electronic devices apart.

5 I'm a _____ of that actor. I love his acting and all the good work he does for charities.

6 Lady Gaga was my _____ when I was younger. I thought she was great.

7 Bobby likes to be the _____ and gets pretty upset when he thinks people are ignoring him.

8 I _____ my older sister when I was a kid and I still think she's the best.

Fame

SB p.61

2 ★☆☆ **Circle the correct words for each definition.**

1 photographers who follow celebrities to take photos of them: *A-list celebrity / paparazzi*

2 at the centre of public attention and interest: *in the limelight / the face of something*

3 avoid attracting attention to yourself: *keep a low profile / celebrity crush*

4 likely to achieve success soon or in the near future: *up-and-coming / A-list celebrity*

5 a strong but temporary feeling of liking a famous person: *paparazzi / celebrity crush*

6 the person who represents a brand: *the face of something / up-and-coming*

7 one of the most famous of famous people: *A-list celebrity / be in the limelight*

8 people who illegally follow and watch someone over a period of time: *paparazzi / stalkers*

3 ★★☆ **Complete the text with words and phrases from Exercise 2.**

This week's ¹_____ is ...

Charli D'Amelio

She's part of a TikTok family with her sister Dixie and their parents Marc and Heidi. Charli is one of TikTok's ²_____ stars and is one of the most-followed people on it. She's not only an amazing dancer, she's also a very funny person with a great sense of humour.

Despite being ³_____ and making videos with stars like J-Lo, Charli and the D'Amelio family try to ⁴_____ . The ⁵_____ don't follow her or take photos and she hasn't had any problems with ⁶_____ . Charli and her family want it to stay that way. For her TikTok viewers, Charli is an ⁷_____ . Dixie and Charli are both ⁸_____ a skincare company and they help promote its brand, but they never promote things they don't agree with. We think that's great! What do you think?

4 ★★★ **Think of a famous person for each question. Give a reason for your answer.**

Who ...

1 really enjoys being in the limelight? _____

2 is an up-and-coming star? _____

3 is a common celebrity crush at the moment?
_____

4 is an A-list celebrity you really admire? _____

5 is the face of your favourite brand? _____
_____

6 likes to keep a low profile? _____

WordWise:
Expressions with *take*

SB p.60

5 ★★☆ **Match the sentence halves.**

1 You don't have to take my word for it – ☐

2 From that look on your face, ☐

3 I know you're worried about your exams, but ☐

4 I wasn't actually talking about you – ☐

5 It would be nice if Dad took an interest in my life – ☐

6 It's great that you've got a new hobby, but ☐

a I take it that you don't like my new haircut.

b don't take everything so personally all the time.

c he has no idea what I'm up to half of the time.

d you need to find something to take your mind off them for a while.

e try not to let it take over your life.

f ask Mrs Page if you don't believe me.

REFERENCE

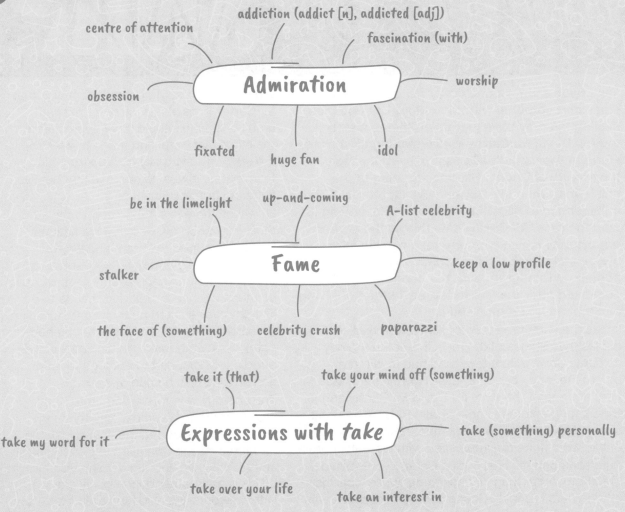

Admiration
- addiction (addict [n], addicted [adj])
- centre of attention
- fascination (with)
- worship
- obsession
- idol
- fixated
- huge fan

Fame
- be in the limelight
- up-and-coming
- A-list celebrity
- keep a low profile
- stalker
- paparazzi
- the face of (something)
- celebrity crush

Expressions with *take*
- take it (that)
- take your mind off (something)
- take my word for it
- take (something) personally
- take over your life
- take an interest in

VOCABULARY EXTRA

1 Read the text and underline six phrasal verbs associated with fame.

Do you want to break into the world of social media and be a big star? If you want your next video to take off, follow these simple steps.

1. Why not take up something new that will add something to your videos? Try singing while you're dancing or cooking.
2. Always tell the truth. Never make up stories that aren't true. Viewers want to watch and learn about the real you.
3. It's OK to turn down requests or offers to be brand ambassadors. If you don't feel comfortable, don't do it!
4. When it's time for your next video to come out, post something short and interesting before it comes out so your followers want to watch it!

2 Match the phrasal verbs in Exercise 1 with the definitions.

1 to refuse to accept or agree to something
_____

2 to invent a story or an excuse
_____

3 a book, record, film, video, etc. becomes available for people to buy or see
_____

4 to suddenly start to be successful or popular
_____

5 to begin to do something
_____

6 to begin working in a new business or area
_____

3 Write three more tips for being successful on social media. Use phrasal verbs from Exercise 1.

1 _____
2 _____
3 _____

THINK BEFORE YOU SNAP

Fans have always done crazy things to get up close and personal with their idols, but one Irish cycling fan may have just taken things a step too far. David McCarthy was watching the third stage of the Giro d'Italia as it passed through the streets of Dublin. He was standing at the finish line, when the German cyclist Marcel Kittel collapsed in exhaustion in front of him, having just won the race. McCarthy saw this as the perfect opportunity to run over and take a selfie with the overwhelmed cyclist, which he immediately posted on Instagram with the caption 'Kittel collapsed after the line today, so instead of giving him a hand up I took a selfie.'

It was the end of the tour for Kittel, who had won the last two stages of the race. The following day he came down with a fever and had to withdraw before the race headed to Italy. However, this was far from the end of the story for David McCarthy and it wasn't long before his post attracted large amounts of negative comments. It seemed that the general public were none too impressed with his selfish selfie.

Australian professional cyclist Cadel Evans called the photo 'more than inconsiderate' while local Irish cycling hero Nicholas Roche commented that it was 'not very respectful and definitely not very funny.' Other comments posted on his account were far less friendly. 'Pity there's no photo where Kittel actually punches him' one person wrote; 'Probably meant as funny. I find this quite disturbing,' wrote another.

What annoyed some people more was that McCarthy himself is a junior cyclist with ambitions, who should have appreciated the effort that Kittel had made to win the stage with virtually no help from his teammates. It was no surprise that he was suffering from exhaustion.

However, there is a happy end to the story. McCarthy soon realised that his actions had overstepped the mark and wrote an apology to the German rider in which he explained that he had never meant to cause so much offence and added that he had just got over-excited by the whole occasion. He said that he now realised that he had been completely wrong in his actions and offered a wholehearted apology to Kittel and anyone else he had offended.

The apology was forwarded on to Kittel, who seemed to be able to see the funny side. He responded to the young Irish fan about the lessons we learn in life, adding a story of his own about a time he was caught by his grandmother dangerously playing with fireworks. He also reminded McCarthy about how brutal social media can be. Hopefully, McCarthy has learned his lesson and will think twice in the future about how and when he takes a selfie.

READING

1 Read the newspaper article. What caused offence – a professional cyclist, a selfie or a comedian?

2 Read the article again. Mark the sentences T (true), F (false) or DS (doesn't say).

1 Marcel Kittel failed to finish the race in Dublin ☐
2 McCarthy asked Kittel if he could take a photo. ☐
3 The Giro d'Italia that year involved more than one country. ☐
4 McCarthy soon learned that most people didn't share his sense of humour over the incident. ☐
5 Roche persuaded McCarthy to write an apology. ☐
6 McCarthy was reluctant to apologise. ☐
7 McCarthy sent his apology directly to Kittel. ☐
8 Kittel was able to empathise with McCarthy. ☐

3 **CRITICAL THINKING** Read the opinions about McCarthy's actions. Tick (✓) the ones that agree with what he did. What is your opinion?

1 McCarthy is a selfish individual, he isn't a fan. ☐
2 I'd have done the same if I could have been at the race. Good for you, David. ☐
3 You didn't need to apologise, David, but well done for doing that! ☐
4 It's people like this that give fans a bad name. Learn some manners. ☐

My opinion: _____

4 Choose one of the options and write a short paragraph.

• Imagine you are McCarthy. Write your apology.
• Write a short text about a time you had to make an apology.

DEVELOPING *Writing*

Writing an essay

1 **INPUT** **Read the essay. Complete the sentence to sum up the writer's conclusion.**

The writer thinks that we have enough

_____

> Celebrities deserve their privacy. Discuss the pros and cons of having special laws to protect the privacy of celebrities. Give your reasons.
>
> Celebrities are people like everyone else and ⁰*they* feel emotions in the same way as other people. Being the centre of attention can create unwanted intrusion from the paparazzi, social media and newspapers. However, whether they are royalty, singers, actors or sports stars, they deserve protection from being followed and having ¹*their* photo taken all the time. If there were special laws to protect them and their families, ²*they* would protect their privacy. They might not want to live every minute of their life in the public eye or be the centre of attention all the time. How would you feel if someone took your photo every time you stepped out of your house and ³*it* appeared on social media within minutes? After a while, ⁴*that* must get really tiresome.
>
> For some people, the existing laws for privacy, stalking and theft are enough. If we create different laws for celebrities, then they might feel like they can do whatever they want. Being a celebrity is a job like any other job; ⁵*it* is just in the public eye more and they should accept ⁶*that*. They might be rich and famous, but they should not get special laws to protect them. Also, if there were special laws, then ⁷*others* might say that it creates more laws to be broken.
>
> In conclusion, I think we already have enough laws to protect celebrities and we don't need any more. Famous people have a right to some privacy and the paparazzi have a responsibility to respect the privacy of the people they are photographing.

2 **Read the essay again and answer the questions.**

1 How does the writer describe celebrities?

_____

2 What type of celebrities does the writer mention?

_____

3 How would special laws help celebrities?

_____

4 What does the writer think must get tiring for celebrities?

_____

5 What might happen if there were special laws?

_____

3 **ANALYSE** **Look at the words in italics in the essay. What does each one refer to?**

0 _they – celebrities_

1 _____

2 _____

3 _____

4 _____

5 _____

6 _____

7 _____

4 **PLAN** **Use the essay to complete the plan.**

1 Introduction
Talk about how there are
_____ (keep this short)

2 Pros
- _____
- 'protection' e.g. – _____
- _____ (most important)

3 Cons
- _____
- _____

4 My conclusion
- _____

5 **Brainstorm some personality adjectives to describe what celebrities are like and the positive and negative aspects of being a celebrity.**

adjectives to describe celebrities

positive aspects of being a celebrity

negative aspects of being a celebrity

6 **PRODUCE** **Choose one of the ideas below and write an essay (220–260 words). Use the plan from Exercise 4. Remember to use adjectives from Exercise 5. Make your own checklist.**

- Paparazzi do more harm than good.
- Reality TV shows should be banned.

✔ CHECKLIST

☐ _____
☐ _____
☐ _____
☐ _____
☐ _____

🎧 LISTENING

1 🔊 6.02 **Listen to the conversations and write the names *Ellie*, *Josh* or *Dan* under the photos of what they're talking about. There is one extra picture.**

A _____   C _____

B _____   D _____

2 🔊 6.02 **Listen again and choose the correct answers.**

Conversation 1
1 When did Lana start the project?
  A last night
  B last weekend
  C last week
2 How does Ellie say she feels?
  A sorry and disappointed
  B sad and upset
  C upset and disappointed

Conversation 2
3 How many minutes does Josh need to find his boots?
  A two
  B three
  C twenty
4 Which of these doesn't Dad mention?
  A being tidy
  B leaving things in the same place
  C surfing the internet

Conversation 3
5 What does Dan want Nick to do?
  A help him get to the next stage of a computer game
  B go out with him and his friends
  C learn about computers
6 What advice does Nick give Dan?
  A It's better not to complain about things.
  B That he'll learn more if he does it himself.
  C That the best games are at the next level.

DIALOGUE

1 **Put the words in order to make sentences from the conversations.**

1 got / do / Haven't / else / time / your / anything / you / with / to / ?
_____

2 deal / a / It's / big / actually / quite
_____

3 do / all / seem / you / It's / ever / to
_____

4 really / need / I / this / now / don't / right
_____

5 learn / this / you'll / from / Maybe
_____

6 I / this / got / for / now / time / really haven't / right
_____

7 to / yourself / I / never / you / If / it / learn / for / do / it / do / you'll
_____

8 on / time / your / This / own / you're
_____

PHRASES FOR FLUENCY   → SB p.62

1 **Put the dialogue in the correct order.**

☐ Jay I've looked in my room and it's not there.

☐ Jay That's not true, Mum. I've got loads of other interests.

☐ Jay You might have told me this would turn into a long moan about the computer. Not again!

[1] Jay Have you seen my phone, Mum?

☐ Jay I don't know. Last week maybe.

☐ Jay Come on, Mum. It's not that bad.

☐ Mum Actually it is. Just out of curiosity, when was the last time you tidied it?

☐ Mum No, but might it be in your room by any chance?

☐ Mum Yes, like playing on your phone. But I guess at least you won't be doing that for a while.

☐ Mum I'm just saying it's all you ever seem to do.

☐ Mum Fat chance you could find anything in your room, it's such a mess.

☐ Mum More like last year. If you spent less time on your computer and more time tidying, for a change, you wouldn't keep losing things.

2 **Write a short dialogue (8–10 lines) between a parent and their son/daughter. Include at least two examples of complaining and two of responding to complaints.**

C1 Advanced

1 You are going to read an extract from a magazine article. Six paragraphs have been removed from the extract. Choose from the paragraphs A–G the one which fits each gap (1–6). There is one extra paragraph which you do not need to use.

On the Road with Rosie

Rosie Swale Pope chose to spend Christmas Day 2020 alone. That was the day she walked into the village of John O'Groats in Scotland, the most northerly point on the British mainland. Behind her was the little trailer-cum-home that she'd literally dragged across the length of Britain from Land's End in the far southwest. 'That's when I turned on my solar panel, plugged in my phone and called all my family and friends', the 74-year-old told me. 'It was wonderful.' The last time I'd spoken to Rosie, in late March of that same year, she'd been confined to a deserted hotel in the hills of Safranbolu in Turkey. The adventurer and writer had been in the middle of an unsupported running expedition from her home in England to Kathmandu in Nepal when the coronavirus pandemic struck.

1 _____

When her visa eventually expired, however, she had no choice but to fly back home, arriving in June and going into quarantine. She still hoped to fly back to Turkey to continue her 5,300-mile journey through 18 countries, to raise money for *Phase Worldwide*, a charity that supports rural communities in Nepal.

2 _____

'Sometimes you can't do what you're meant to do, but you can always do something.' she recalls about that decision. With her lightweight carbon-fibre trailer still stuck at the Turkish hotel, she had to use her back-up vehicle, a heavier one made of fibreglass. She got a lift in a van to Land's End and set off running on 12 July.

3 _____

Although she saw the spontaneous adventure as a 1500-kilometre training run while she waited to complete her bigger challenge, it later occurred to her that it might also be the first phase of an alternative route back to Nepal — she decided to catch a cargo ship or ferry from Scotland to Norway, and then try to reach Kathmandu via Finland, Russia and China.

4 _____

But Rosie Swale Pope isn't familiar with ideas like self-doubt or giving up. In a globetrotting career as a writer and adventurer, she has completed ultra-marathons in the Sahara, sailed solo across the Atlantic, ridden the length of Chile on horseback and raised hundreds of thousands of pounds for charity in sponsorship.

5 _____

Yet it was in her own country, on an unplanned jaunt by her standards, that she may end up feeling most fulfilled. Her plans for the trip were too rushed to alert Guinness World Records, but she hopes to have collected enough evidence on her phone to be recognised as the oldest woman to complete the trip on foot – her first entry in that famous listing.

6 _____

Rosie had to wait out a travel ban in Scotland before continuing with her trip, but saw this as a chance to work on her latest book. The adventurer's resilience and patience in the face of age, discomfort and thwarted plans are, perhaps, a universal lesson. As she says: 'You can always do something.'

A But as days turned to weeks, and with no sure sign that she'd be able to go back to Turkey and complete the three-thousand remaining miles, she had another, only slightly less adventurous thought. There was always Britain itself. It had always been her dream to run from one end to the other and now she had the chance.

B Clearly, simply reaching one goal wasn't enough for Rosie. If anyone else were to come up with such outlandish plans in the grip of a global pandemic whilst nearing the middle of their eighth decade, you'd think they were being unrealistic.

C Despite those setbacks, there were brighter moments. 'One woman came up to me at midnight when I was camped in a muddy roadside layby,' she says. 'We chatted and she came back an hour later with an amazing meal she'd prepared.'

D Mostly camping in the 110kg trailer, and managing about sixteen kilometres a day, she kept going until she reached her destination. 'I didn't take all my clothes off for several weeks,' says Rosie, who faced days on end of rain on her route.

E Rosie spent more than two months cooking spaghetti on her camping stove and running up and down the stairs of the locked-down building in an attempt to stay fit. Her tiny red trailer, which held all her supplies and space for sleeping, sat in the empty car park.

F Perhaps the most ambitious of these trips saw her run around the world, clocking up almost 32,000 kilometres over five years and passing through northern Europe, Russia, Alaska, Canada and the US whilst dragging her own supplies. She nearly froze to death in Alaska and was chased by wolves in Siberia. 'When you've had icicles for earrings, you're prepared for anything,' she says.

G Such an achievement, however, would also be a reminder that she may not have many continent-crossing years left in her. 'I'm fit and 74, and hope to skip along when I'm 94, but nothing is certain,' she says.

CONSOLIDATION

🎧 LISTENING

1 🔊 6.03 **Listen and complete the notes.**

> **Name:** Tom Lackey
>
> **Current Age:** ¹_____
>
> **Stunt:** ²_____
>
> **Departure:** Castle Kennedy in
> ³_____
>
> **Arrival:** City of Derry Airport in
> ⁴_____
>
> **Time taken:**
> ⁵_____
>
> **World record set earlier in the same year:** ⁶_____
>
> **In 2005:** ⁷_____

2 🔊 6.03 **Listen again and answer the questions.**

1 What year was the aircraft used built in?
_____

2 How long has Mr Lackey been wing walking?
_____

3 How old was he when his wife died?
_____

4 How much money has he raised for charity so far?
_____

5 When was he awarded the 'Pride of Britain'?
_____

6 How many times did he fly from the UK to France?
_____

7 How old was he when he wing walked on a plane as it looped-the-loop? _____

© GRAMMAR

3 **Circle the correct options.**

1 *Inspiring / Inspired* by the astronomy lecture, I went out and bought a telescope.

2 You *must / can't* be hungry. You haven't eaten all day.

3 I knew it was early because I heard birds *sing / singing*.

4 Having three brothers *can / may* be quite annoying at times. I know from experience.

5 *Cooking / Cooked* Thai food is the way I like to relax.

6 Dad *can't / won't* let me go to the game, so you'll have to go without me.

7 I saw the man *fall / falling* off his bike and ran over to help him.

8 *Feeling / Felt* rather tired, I decided to have an early night.

🅰 VOCABULARY

4 **Complete the sentences with prepositions.**

1 A lot of people have a fascination _____ watching TikTok videos.

2 Who's the new face _____ that sports brand? Is it a basketball player?

3 I get a real kick _____ of playing tennis. It's just the best sport.

4 Social media is great but you do need to be careful not to let it take _____ your life.

5 I don't want to pour cold water _____ your idea but I think we need to look at it in more detail.

6 Don't take my word _____ it. Ask Mr Thomas.

7 You'll be _____ hot water with your parents if you do that.

8 Why don't you watch a film to help take your mind _____ your exams for a while?

5 **Replace the words in italics with the words in the list.**

> celebrity crush on | centre of attention
> daredevil | hot under the collar
> huge fan of | idol | paparazzi | stunts

1 There were lots of *dangerous action pieces* in the film.
_____

2 He couldn't believe his eyes. He opened the door and *the photographers* took his picture.
_____

3 Who do you have a *strong, but temporary feeling of liking* for at the moment?
_____

4 Everywhere she goes she wants to be the *focus of everything*.
_____

5 I love everything he does. He's my *star*.
_____

6 He's not scared to take risks. He's a *man who fears nothing*.
_____

7 He got *embarrassed and angry* when I suggested he wasn't a celebrity.
_____

8 Jed loves sitcoms. He is a *person who knows everything about it*.
_____

DIALOGUE

6 Complete the dialogue with the words in the list. There are two you do not need.

accept | come | do | give | point | see | suppose | talk

Ed Mountain biking, mountain biking. It's all you ever ¹_____ about.

Maya ²_____ on, Ed. It's my hobby. What's the problem?

Ed But it's all you do. Haven't you got anything else to ³_____ with your time?

Maya That's not true. I don't ⁴_____ that. I've got plenty of other hobbies.

Ed Like what?

Maya Well, I'm in the girls' football team at school, I play the saxophone in the school band, I'm a member of the school eco council, I help out at the old people's home at the weekend. Do you want me to go on?

Ed OK, ⁵_____ taken. But I do think you spend too much time on your mountain bike.

Maya Don't get so hot under the collar about it. The way I ⁶_____ it is this. I know you're not a risk-taker but really there aren't too many risks. You should come cycling with me one day and see for yourself.

📖 READING

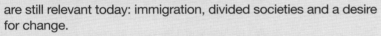

Hamilton or Hamilteen?

Hamilton is Lin-Manuel Miranda's hit Broadway musical show combining hip-hop, rap, jazz and R&B with great acting. It tells the true story of Alexander Hamilton with themes that are still relevant today: immigration, divided societies and a desire for change.

Josie is 17 and she's a Hamilteen. Having studied American history at school this year, she really got into it after her teacher used a video of part of *Hamilton* in class. It was like a living history lesson. She may not have seen *Hamilton* live, but she knows everything about it except what it's like to see it live. Playing the music non-stop means that she knows the lyrics off by heart and singing the songs is one of her favourite things to do.

And it's not just girls who are superfans – teenage boys are hooked, too. They admire the young men who are depicted as strong and brave. They love the songs and the lyrics, too. Jamie is a super fan who made a special journey to New York City and visited all the places mentioned in the musical. He loves the rap battles and can rap them faster than any of his friends. He practises regularly with a group of Hamilteens and they sometimes perform for family and friends. His favourite rap is *Guns and Ships* – it's one of the fastest raps in Broadway theatre history and it's become a challenge for superfans to rap it perfectly. Rapping 19 words in three seconds is quite an audacious feat!

Spending a lot of time in front of a screen can often be a bad thing, but even parents of Hamilteens don't mind – listening to the soundtrack or watching the show means teenagers are using their imaginations as they're listening. Having picked up their phones or tablets, they have shared videos of themselves rapping 19 words in three seconds. Surely that can't be a bad thing?

As luck would have it, *Hamilton* has now started streaming on TV so Josie and Jamie can see it. A dream come true for superfans though, would be to go to Broadway and see it live. Maybe one day …

7 Read the article and answer the questions.

1 What is *Hamilton*?

_____
_____
_____

2 What is a Hamilteen?

_____
_____
_____

3 What inspired Josie to become a Hamilteen?

_____
_____
_____

4 What do boys like about *Hamilton*?

_____
_____
_____

5 How can superfans now see the show?

_____
_____
_____

✏️ WRITING

8 Imagine you are a superfan. Write a letter (180–200 words) to the person you are a superfan of and explain why you like and admire them.

7 A THING OF BEAUTY?

Grammar video

▶18

G GRAMMAR

Substitution (*the ones, so, that of, do*) → SB p.68

1 ⭐☆☆ **Circle the correct verbs.**

  1 **A** Do you think this class will help us to get fit?
     B I hope *so / it*.

  2 **A** Are you finding the Insanity workout difficult?
     B Yes, a bit. There are some people who are really good at it and *those / that* who aren't.

  3 **A** A lot of our friends used to go to pilates classes.
     B A lot of people still *so / do*.

  4 **A** I'd never heard of zorbing before I came to this class.
     B *So / Neither* had we.

  5 **A** I think the Tough Mudder will be really popular.
     B I reckon *so / one*.

  6 **A** I have one goal, *those / that* of running a ten kilometre race.
     B Me, too.

2 ⭐⭐☆ **Complete the dialogue with the words in the list.**

> do | nor | so | the one | those

Arlo What's Surf Set? I've never heard of it.

Beth ¹_____ have I. You're ²_____ who usually knows about all the latest fitness trends. Is it water aerobics classes? Helena tried one of ³_____ . She said it was quite good.

Arlo No, I don't think ⁴_____ . I'll read out what it says. You stand on a mechanical surfboard that moves and shakes. You have to use your 'core balance' while doing a series of exercises such as squats and jumps.

Beth I think it might be good.

Arlo I ⁵_____ , too.

3 ⭐⭐⭐ **Complete the dialogues so they are true for you. Then justify your answers.**

> I do / Nor do I | I have / Neither have I
> I reckon so / don't reckon so
> I think so / don't think so | People still do
> So can I / I can't | So do I / I don't

  0 **A** I think everyone should do at least half an hour of exercise a day.
     You So do I. Then everybody would be much healthier.

  1 **A** I don't think sugary, fizzy drinks are good for you.
     You _____
           _____

  2 **A** Is it easy for people to learn to run using an app?
     You _____

  3 **A** I've never tried an exercise game.
     You _____

  4 **A** I reckon you'd be good at yoga.
     You _____
           _____

  5 **A** I think hula-hooping would be good fun.
     You _____
           _____

  6 **A** I can stand on my head.
     You _____
           _____

4 ⭐⭐⭐ **Write sentences comparing the past and the present. Use the words in brackets. You can compare: cars, clothes, computers, food, video games.**

  0 (that) *Music listened to today is much more fast-paced than that* _____ listened to 50 years ago.

  1 (that) _____
     _____ eaten 100 years ago.

  2 (those) _____
     _____ driven 50 years ago.

  3 (that) _____
     _____ worn 40 years ago.

  4 (those) _____
     _____ used 30 years ago.

  5 (those) _____
     _____ played 20 years ago.

Ellipsis

 SB p.69

5 ★☆☆ **Match the long sentences (1–7) with the short sentences (a–h). Then complete the long sentences.**

0 _____Would you like_____ another coffee? ☐ C

1 _____ love one. ☐

2 _____ fancy playing a game of tennis? ☐

3 _____ time for a cup of tea? ☐

4 _____ sorry but I can't stay. ☐

5 _____ worry about it. ☐

6 _____ want to listen to another track? ☐

7 _____ seen you here before. ☐

a Not seen you here before.
b Sorry, I can't stay.
c Another coffee?
d No worries.
e Love one.
f Time for a cup of tea?
g Fancy a game of tennis?
h Want to listen to another track?

6 ★★☆ **Write short versions of the sentences.**

0 That's great.
   Great.

1 I love your new haircut.
   _____

2 Would you like to have an ice cream?
   _____

3 Have you got any chocolate?
   _____

4 Have you seen Sam today?
   _____

5 It isn't a problem.
   _____

7 ★★☆ **Cross out the unnecessary words in the answers to the questions.**

1 A Where's Paola?
   B I don't know.

2 A Does Max know the address?
   B I'm not sure.

3 A I've got a new game.
   B That's nice.

4 A How are you?
   B I'm not bad.

5 A Would you like an apple?
   B Yes, please. I would like an apple.

6 A Shall we stay and watch the next film?
   B No, I think we had better go home now.

8 ★★☆ **Circle the correct answers.**

1 A Have you seen any good films recently?
   B *A couple. / Got a couple.*

2 A How do you feel?
   B *Great. / It's great.*

3 A Luis has got into university.
   B *Interest. / Interesting.*

4 A Have you ever been to a Pilates class?
   B *Not today. / Once.*

5 A Would you like some more ice cream?
   B *Love some. / Love one.*

6 A Would you like to come to a football match on Saturday?
   B *Love one. / Love to.*

GET IT RIGHT!

Substitution

Learners often make mistakes with *so* or *either* by omitting them or using *it* instead.

✓ *Do you think I'll pass the exam? I hope so.*

✗ *Do you think I'll pass the exam? I hope.*

Rewrite the sentences using *so*, *either* or *neither*. Some of the sentences are incorrect and some can be shortened.

0 Emily is very fashionable – well, certainly more fashionable than me.

   Emily is very fashionable – well, certainly more so than me.

1 Rebecca thinks Kathryn needs to run greater distances in training if she's going to complete the marathon and she thinks it, too.

   _____

2 Monica hasn't been to a fitness class in ages and Jo hasn't been to a fitness class.

   _____

3 My mum thinks that ripped jeans will soon go out of fashion and my dad certainly hopes it, too!

   _____

4 Mark doesn't like the retro look and so doesn't Finn.

   _____

5 Smartphones have become a must-have and tablets have.

   _____

6 Isaac is going to cut down on his screen time and George is going to cut down on his screen time.

   _____

PRONUNCIATION
Connected speech feature: assimilation **Go to page 120.**

Az VOCABULARY
Fads

→ SB p.68

1 ★☆☆ **Match the words to make expressions.**

1	go out	a	lived
2	bang	b	thing
3	really	c	have
4	short-	d	of fashion
5	a	e	in
6	must-	f	best thing
7	the next	g	on trend

2 ★★☆ **Circle the correct words to complete the statements about fashion.**

FASHION

IN 1990S AMERICA AND BRITAIN

1 In the late 1980s and the early 1990s, bright coloured tops and leg warmers were *bang on trend / short-lived*.

2 Mid 1992 'grunge' fashion became popular and fingerless gloves and ripped jeans were *out of fashion / really in* for men.

3 Aviator-style sunglasses, popularised by the rock star Freddie Mercury, were the *really in / must-have* fashion accessory.

4 Fashions in trousers were often *short-lived / the next best thing* but jeans survived the decade and will do for many more.

5 In the late 1990s, there was a 1970s revival and platform shoes were fashionable. If you didn't have a pair of platform shoes, a pair of knee-high boots were *the next best thing / out of fashion*.

6 In 1995, baggy jeans, tracksuits and 'bomber' jackets were *a thing / short-lived*.

7 By 2000, baggy jeans *were the next best thing / had gone out of fashion*. It wasn't trendy to wear them.

Emotional responses

→ SB p.71

3 ★★☆ **Read the clues and complete the puzzle with the missing words. Find the mystery word.**

(crossword grid with letters P, P, N in the shaded column)

1 It sends _____ down my spine.
2 It sets my heart _____ .
3 It brings a _____ to my face.
4 It brings a _____ to my eye.
5 It makes my heart _____ .
6 It gives me _____ on my arms.
The mystery word is _____ .

4 ★★☆ **Complete the dialogues with expressions from Exercise 3 and your own ideas.**

1 A Do you have a favourite song or piece of music?
You I love _____ (name of song/music). It _____ when I hear the opening chords.

2 A Do you know any sad songs?
You Yes, I do. _____ (name of song). It _____ whenever I listen to it.

3 A Where would you say is the place you feel happiest?
You _____ (name of a place). It _____ whenever I think of it.

4 A Have you ever heard _____ (name of a singer) sing?
You Yes, I have. He/She has such an amazing voice. I _____ whenever I listen to him/her sing.

5 A Can you think of anything scary or anything that gives you a thrill?
You _____ .

6 A What makes you smile?
You When I see _____ (name of person/pet). _____ .

REFERENCE
Fads

BANG ON TREND   MUST-HAVE
GO OUT OF FASHION
REALLY IN   SHORT-LIVED   A THING
THE NEXT BEST THING

send shivers down (my) spine — bring a tear to (my) eye

Emotional responses

bring a smile to (my) face

set (my) heart racing

give me goosebumps — make my heart soar

VOCABULARY EXTRA

1 Match the underlined expressions with their definitions.

1 Worried about your <u>sense of style</u>? Contact us and we'll help you work it out and find your best look.

2 Birthday party, graduation, wedding? Want to <u>dress for the occasion</u>? Our personal stylists can help you choose! Email us now to book.

3 We make clothes for you and no one else. We don't do <u>off-the-peg</u> styles. What we do, we do just for you.

4 The celebrities were all <u>dressed to kill</u> on the red carpet last night.

5 Are you <u>a slave to fashion</u>? Don't be! Follow this advice and be yourself.

6 <u>Take pride in your appearance</u> and the rest will follow!

a to wear clothes that are appropriate for a specific event ☐
b to be influenced too much by something in the world of fashion ☐
c to dress well in a way that makes you feel proud and satisfied ☐
d a good awareness of what is in fashion / fashionable ☐
e wearing glamorous clothes to make an impression ☐
f not made for a particular person; made and bought in standard sizes ☐

2 Find the mistake in each sentence. Correct the mistakes.

1 Wow! You look amazing. You're dressed off-the-peg tonight. What's happening?
2 Luca's a slave to the occasion. He must spend all his allowance on clothes.
3 I think it's important to take pride in your sense every day even when you're at home.
4 Do you want an off-the-occasion outfit or one that is made just for you?
5 We should dress for the fashion so we need something appropriate for a wedding.
6 You've got a good sense of appearance. Can you help me choose a new outfit?

3 Answer the questions about you.

1 Are you a slave to fashion? Why? / Why not?
_____
2 Who do you know that has a good sense of style? What's their style like?
_____
3 What's more important for you: to dress for the occasion or just be yourself? Why?
_____

THE PRICE OF BEAUTY

Over the centuries some very dangerous products have been used to follow fashions of the time.

The Secret of a Good Complexion
TO ALL WOMEN WHO DESIRE BEAUTY.

Until further notice we will send you a 30-day daily treatment of Dr. Campbell's Safe Arsenic Complexion Wafers and a 30-day daily treatment of Fould's Medicated Arsenic Soap FOR ONE DOLLAR.

These world-famous preparations are a never failing remedy for bad blood, pimples, freckles, blackheads, moth patches, liver spots, acne, redness of face or nose, wrinkles, dark rings under the eyes, and all other blemishes, whether on the face, neck, arms or body. They brighten and beautify the complexion as no other remedies on earth can, and they do it in a very short time. They impart to the complexion the most exquisite fairness, make the skin clear, soft and velvety. Until further notice we will send you the wafers and soap as stated above for $1.00. After this offer is withdrawn the price will be $1.00 for the wafers and 50c. for the soap. Address or call on

H. B. FOULD, Dept. A, 214 Sixth Ave., New York.
Sold by Druggists Everywhere.

USING LEAD IN MAKE-UP

Queen Elizabeth I of England made it fashionable to have pale skin. In her time, it was considered beautiful to have a very white face, and she used a lead face powder to achieve this look. Lead powder was easy to make and was cheap, so men and women would put thick layers of it onto their faces every day. This achieved the pale, smooth look they wanted, but sadly, the lead in the powder was slowly poisoning them. Symptoms included grey hair, very dry skin, stomach aches, swollen brains and finally, a very painful death.

ARSENIC PILLS AND SOAPS

The use of the poison arsenic for losing weight and improving the skin seems to have begun in the 1850s. James F. W. Johnston, a Scottish agricultural chemist, made arsenic pills famous after he wrote an article about them in his book, *The Chemistry of Common Life*, which was first published in 1855. After this, adverts began to appear for arsenic pills and soaps.

The pills made the skin pale by destroying red blood cells. In July 1880, there was an article in an American newspaper, the *Indianapolis Sentinel*, about a young lady who had gradually lost her sight as a result of taking arsenic pills. People also died taking the pills. In 1911, 18-year-old Hildegarde Walton of St Louis died after taking several boxes of pills to clear up the spots on her face.

DEADLY NIGHTSHADE EYE DROPS

The poisonous plant, deadly nightshade (or belladonna), was used by women in eye drops from Roman times until the late 19th century. It made the eyes look more attractive. Unfortunately, deadly nightshade is one of the most poisonous plants on the planet. Using these eye drops caused sight problems and blindness. It also caused other serious health problems and eventually, death.

DANGEROUS DIET PILLS TODAY

Eloise Aimee Parry, a 21-year-old university student in the UK, bought some slimming pills on the internet. When she started to feel unwell, she drove herself to hospital. She told the doctors what she had taken. The pills contained a dangerous ingredient, DNP. Eloise tragically died.

We now live in the 21st century and our medical knowledge has improved, but have things changed? It would seem not. It seems that the price that some people are willing to pay for beauty is extremely high – sometimes even their lives. Attracted by cheap prices and claims of success, many people are buying unregulated and dangerous health and beauty products over the internet and unfortunately, pay for them with their lives. Be aware of the dangers.

📖 READING

1 Read the article quickly and find out what each of these toxins was used in.

> arsenic | deadly nightshade | DNP | lead

2 Read the article again. Then write the questions for these answers.

1 _____ ?
Queen Elizabeth I.

2 _____ ?
Grey hair, very dry skin, stomach aches, swollen brains, and finally a very painful death.

3 _____ ?
Because the red blood cells had been destroyed.

4 _____ ?
It is one of the most poisonous plants.

5 _____ ?
She drove herself.

6 _____ ?
People are drawn by the cheap prices and claims of success.

3 CRITICAL THINKING Read problem 1 and the three solutions (A–C). Which solution do you think is best? Why? Give reasons. Then read problem 2 and write your own solution.

1 Your friend has made their own natural hair dye and wants to sell it online.

A What's the problem? It's a great idea and they should start selling it immediately.

B You're not sure this is the best idea. It might be better to start with friends and family first and check there aren't any problems with it.

C There is potential in the idea, but it's a complicated process to sell things online. Suggest they try to sell it to a local shop.

2 You want to start giving exercise classes online and charge people for each session. You don't have any qualifications.

4 Write a dialogue (8–10 lines) between two friends.

• Friend A wants to buy a 'miracle cure' on the internet.

• Friend B wants to convince him/her of the dangers and stop him/her from buying it.

DEVELOPING Writing

Writing a letter of complaint

1 INPUT **Read the letter of complaint. What is the complaint about?**

> The Manager
> Revitalise Hair & Beauty Products
> PO Box 1065
> London
> UK
>
> Dear Sir/Madam,
>
> I am writing to you to complain about one of your products, Vita-Hair shampoo and conditioner, which I recently purchased from your website. I feel that the language used in the advertisement for the product is very misleading.
>
> The advertisement claims that it is 'a revolutionary new product', that after just one use will give me 'fuller, thicker hair'. That's rubbish! I have been using Vita-Hair for three months now and I haven't noticed any difference in the thickness of my hair.
>
> Secondly, the advertisement asks, 'Have you always dreamed of having shiny healthy hair?' Then, it promises, 'Vita-Hair will give you that dream hair.' In fact, my friends and family say my hair has become dull and lifeless. My mum even asked me if I was ill. This is the worst shampoo I've ever tried.
>
> Finally, according to the advertisement, there are only natural oils in the shampoo and conditioner. After receiving the product in the post, I checked the list of ingredients on the back of the bottles and I found that there are several chemicals in the shampoo and conditioner. How can you lie to people like that?
>
> The product was on offer for a limited length of time so unfortunately, I bought it. I feel that your advertisement for the product is misleading and I would like a refund.
>
> Please let me know as soon as possible what you propose to do.
>
> Yours faithfully,
>
> *Maria Brydon*

2 ANALYSE **Complete the reasons Maria gives for her complaint.**

1 The advert claims to _____

_____

After three months, Maria _____

2 The advert promises to _____

_____

The shampoo makes _____

3 The advert says that _____

_____

The shampoo contains _____

3 **Underline three sentences in the letter that express too much anger or are inappropriate.**

4 PLAN **You are going to write a letter of complaint about a product you have recently bought. Choose from the ideas below or use your own idea. Think about the problems and make notes.**

> a beauty product | a game
> an electronic item | an exercise app

WRITING TIP: A LETTER OF COMPLAINT

- Express your unhappiness with the product, but be polite and reasonable.
- Include language of persuasion. Quote what the advertisement said.
- Begin a new paragraph for each main point. Be concise.
- State clearly what you would like to be done.

5 PRODUCE **Write a letter of complaint (220–260 words). Use your ideas from Exercise 4 and the information in the Writing tip. Write your own checklist.**

✓ CHECKLIST

☐ _____
☐ _____
☐ _____
☐ _____
☐ _____

🎧 LISTENING

1 🔊 **7.02** Listen to a conversation between Kit and Erin. Complete the definition of steampunk.

> **steampunk** _____
> _____
> _____

2 🔊 **7.02** Look at the pictures. Which of these things do they mention? Listen again and check.

1 ☐   4 ☐

2 ☐   5 ☐

3 ☐

3 🔊 **7.02** Listen again and answer the questions.

1 Why does steampunk use the word 'steam'?
_____

2 How did Kit learn to make steampunk accessories?
_____

3 Why did Kit decide to make his own steampunk outfits?
_____

4 How does he describe his hat to Erin?
_____

5 What does Erin suggest Kit should do?
_____

DIALOGUE

1 Complete the advertising speeches with the phrases in the list.

> have you always dreamed | imagine
> one million people worldwide
> revolutionary new | strongly recommend
> this brand new | this offer is limited
> we understand that

KEEP ON RUNNING! 🏃

¹_____ of running a marathon? Then let us help you to make your dream come true. ²_____ training to run 42.19 km isn't easy and we ³_____ that you pay a visit to your doctor before you start training. Once you have the go ahead from your doctor, you can ease your way into training with a few walks and gentle jogs. Develop your training routine at a natural and healthy pace.

ALL EYES ON YOU

Make sure all eyes are on you with our fantastic selection of sunglasses at amazingly low prices. Whatever your style, we've got just the sunglasses for you. Last year, ⁴_____ chose to wear our sunglasses. All our sunglasses offer a high level of UV protection as well as being stylish. Try our dark blue retro square sunglasses for only £59.99.
Hurry! ⁵_____ and will end on Friday.

THE BIKE IN A BACKPACK

The *Backpacker* is a ⁶_____ design for bikes. It folds into a special backpack and it's made of light-weight metal and it has a small motor to help you on those steep hills. ⁷_____ design makes the bike a lot more comfortable to ride. ⁸_____ being able to ride for hours without feeling at all tired!

2 Write an advertising speech recommending a product. Use phrases from Exercise 1 and the ideas in the list.

> a new beauty product | a sugar-free drink
> an exercise game | some new exercise equipment

C1 Advanced

READING AND USE OF ENGLISH
Part 4: Key word transformation

⟶ SB p.28

EXAM GUIDE:

In Part 4 of the Reading and Use of English exam, there are six questions. Each question has a sentence, followed by a key word and a gapped sentence. You must complete the gaps with three to six words, including the key word given, so that the second sentence has the same meaning as the first.

- Look carefully at the structure of the original sentence.
- Check the tense.
- Look at the words around the gap in the second sentence. Ask yourself questions: What verbs go with the preposition or what prepositions go with the word? Is it followed by an infinitive or a gerund?
- To practise for the test, always check the synonyms of words and expressions you look up in your dictionary.

1 **For questions 1–6, complete the second sentence so that it has a similar meaning to the first sentence, using the word given. Do not change the word given. You must use between three and six words, including the word given.**

Here is an example (0)

0 In Lord Byron's day, everyone thought that poets should look pale and thin.

EXPECTED

In Lord Byron's day, poets ____*were expected to be*____ pale and thin in appearance.

1 Byron followed a very strict diet because he didn't want his weight to increase.

AVOID

Byron followed a very strict diet in order _____ on weight.

2 Byron only ate a thin slice of bread and a cup of tea for breakfast.

EXCEPT

Byron _____ a thin slice of bread and a cup of tea for breakfast.

3 By 1822, Byron was in a poor state of health, which was caused by his dieting.

RESULT

By 1822, Byron was in a poor state of health _____ his dieting.

4 Byron knew that a poor diet had made him ill.

AWARE

Bryon _____ had been caused by a poor diet.

5 Everyone could see that Byron weighed much less than he had previously.

DEAL

It was evident that Byron had _____ of weight.

6 Many young people thought that Lord Byron was a good role model.

REGARDED

Lord Byron _____ a good role model by young people.

8 CRACKING THE CODE

▶20 Grammar video

Ⓖ GRAMMAR
Relative clauses with determiners and prepositions → SB p.76

1 ★★☆ **Match the pictures with the sentences. Then circle the correct options.**

 A
 D
 B
 E
 C
 F

These are photographs of our family from my grandmother's photo album.

1 The tall fat man in this picture is my grandfather, *compared to which / compared to whom* my father beside him is quite thin, really.

2 There are five children in this photo, *all of which / all of whom* are my cousins.

3 There are several older women in this photo, *one of whom / some of whom* are my grandmother's aunts.

4 Here's my grandfather's little old car, *compared to which / compared to whom* our modern car is huge.

5 Here's a picture of several old dolls, *one of which / some of which* was my grandmother's when she was a child.

6 The woman sitting in this picture is holding two babies, *one of whom / both of whom* is me!

2 ★★☆ **Complete the sentences with phrases from the list.**

> both of which | compared to which | in which case
> most of which | neither of which | none of whom
> one of which

1 My sister speaks Spanish and Portuguese, _____ I find very difficult.

2 My father lent me some books, _____ is in German, so I can't read it.

3 Ed went to Thailand with his friends, _____ speak Thai, so they had difficulty getting around.

4 Tammy is studying Hungarian, _____ English is really very simple.

5 Carlos might go and work in Hong Kong, _____ he will have to learn some Chinese.

6 My dad speaks five languages, _____ are from his home country, India.

7 My new flatmate speaks Polish and Dutch, _____ I'd heard before, but I want to learn them now.

3 ★★★ **Complete the sentences with a determiner from list A, *whom* or *which* and a phrase from list B.**

A
> many of | most of | most of | none of
> none of | one of | some of

B
> agreed with the proposal, but others didn't. |
> are free, but you have to pay for most. |
> ever got married. | plays basketball professionally. |
> said they could come. |
> she bought on the internet. | won the prize.

1 Jason is really disappointed. He bought ten lottery tickets,
_____

2 Dani is very happy. She invited a lot of friends,
_____

3 Scott has a lot of very tall cousins,
_____

4 My grandmother lived with her six sisters,
_____

5 Sue has dozens of model frogs,
_____

6 Hundreds of people answered the survey,
_____

7 There are some interesting places to visit in the city,
_____

however, wherever, whatever, etc.

→ SB p.77

4 ★★☆ Complete the gaps with *however, wherever, whenever, whoever* or *whatever*.

1 _____ you go in the world, English can be useful.

2 Brazilian people are very kind. _____ badly you speak Portuguese, they're happy you're making the effort.

3 My brother and I invented a secret language which we used _____ we didn't want our parents to understand us.

4 We can speak English or French, _____ you're most comfortable with.

5 _____ you do, don't comment on her spelling. She knows it isn't good.

6 Three dictionaries as prizes will be awarded to _____ gets the most correct answers.

7 Pierre turns on the subtitles _____ a film is in English.

8 _____ long you study a language, there is always more to learn.

5 ★★☆ Complete the gaps with a *wh-* word or an *-ever* word.

1 It was June _____ I visited the island.

2 The people in the village _____ I stayed were really nice to me.

3 _____ I went on the island everyone was friendly.

4 Fortunately there were a lot of people _____ spoke English.

5 The hostel provided me with _____ I wanted – guidebooks, maps, etc. Anything!

6 There were so many places to visit on the island that I had some difficulty deciding _____ to do first.

7 The beaches are at their best in the morning when they're quiet, but they're beautiful _____ you go there.

8 The people are proud of their history. _____ I spoke to, they knew a lot.

6 ★★★ Rewrite the extract from a letter, replacing the underlined phrases with phrases including an *-ever* word.

[1]<u>It doesn't matter what</u> you decide to do with your life, you need to have languages behind you. [2]<u>It's not important where</u> you go, you will have to communicate with people. When I was at school, [3]<u>any and every person who</u> was studying sciences also had to study a language. I know I found it very helpful [4]<u>at any time</u> I was in France. I was always able to contribute to a conversation, [5]<u>it didn't matter what</u> it was about. So try to learn a language – or two, or three! [6]<u>It doesn't matter how</u> difficult it seems at the time, your efforts will be rewarded. [7]<u>It's not important where</u> you study, how much you learn depends on you.

So, work hard, have fun and be successful! And good luck – Bonne chance! Buena suerte! Viel Gluck! Zhù nǐ hǎo yùn! In bocca al lupo!

GET IT RIGHT!

however, wherever, whatever, etc.

Learners often omit *-ever* from *however, wherever, whatever,* etc. sentences.

✓ *Whichever way I choose to go always seems to be the wrong way!*

✗ ~~Which~~ *way I choose to go always seems to be the wrong way!*

Tick (✓) the sentences which are correct and rewrite the incorrect ones.

1 It's important to who's receiving it. ☐
_____

2 I didn't quite get what he said, but what he did say I'm not interested. ☐
_____

3 Who said that my accent was too strong to understand? ☐
_____

4 Whatever I do, it always seems to be wrong! ☐
_____

5 I'm going to try to learn either Japanese or Chinese – I'll choose which course is cheaper. ☐
_____

6 How fluent you may be, there will always be someone who doesn't follow you. ☐
_____

VOCABULARY
Language and communication

→ SB p.76

1 ★☆☆ **Circle the correct options.**

1 You can communicate a lot using *face / facial* expressions.

2 Someone who has spoken a certain language since they were born is a *native / first* speaker.

3 A movement you make with your hand(s) is a *gesture / body* language.

4 They use different words in that part of the country – it's a very different *dialect / barrier*.

5 He spoke so fast that he was *incomprehensible / broken*.

6 Some sounds in another language can be hard to *accent / pronounce*.

7 We misunderstood each other totally – it was a complete communication *breakdown / barrier*.

8 I like listening to French people speaking English – I think their *dialect / accent* is wonderful!

9 I'd forgotten all the German I'd learned at school so I ended up speaking *broken / body language* German.

10 Your body *expression / language* tells people a lot about what you're really thinking.

2 ★★☆ **Complete the sentences with a word or phrase from page 76 of the Student's Book.**

1 I couldn't understand a word of what she was saying – it was completely _____ to me.

2 What's the _____ of people who are born in Quebec – French or English?

3 I didn't mean that. She completely _____ me.

4 The biggest problem for Selina when she moved to Berlin was the _____ because she didn't speak German.

5 Sometimes, if you can't speak the language, a _____ with your hands will help.

6 However hard I tried, I couldn't _____ understood.

7 When we were in Japan, our tour guide had to _____ for us all the time because we didn't speak any Japanese.

8 It's hard to _____ people from that area because they pronounce words in a very different way.

9 They just stopped talking or listening to each other – it was a total _____ .

10 I could tell she wasn't happy to see me – her _____ made it very clear, for example, when she crossed her arms.

Personality (2)

→ SB p.79

3 ★☆☆ **Match the words (1–8) with the definitions (a–h).**

1 forceful ☐   5 modest ☐
2 self-assured ☐   6 expressive ☐
3 assertive ☐   7 self-conscious ☐
4 conceited ☐   8 impulsive ☐

a stating your opinions strongly and demanding action or answers

b not saying much about yourself or your abilities or achievements

c having confidence in your own abilities

d not afraid to say what you want or believe

e showing what you think or feel

f being too proud of yourself or your actions and abilities

g nervous or uncomfortable because you're worried about what others think about you

h suddenly deciding to do something and not thinking much about the result

4 ★★☆ **Write an adjective to describe each person.**

0 'Do you think this shirt looks alright? Is it the wrong colour for me?' ___*self-conscious*___

1 'Winning the competition wasn't a big deal. I think I just got lucky.' _____

2 'Hey! Let's not go to the cinema tonight – let's just get on a train and go somewhere, anywhere!' _____

3 'Well, I'm sorry but I really disagree with you about that.' _____

4 'I think I'll be OK in the interview – I'll be able to answer their questions, I reckon.' _____

5 'His words and gestures make it easy to understand how he's feeling.' _____

6 'Well you made a mistake and you have to do something about it – now!' _____

7 'There's no doubt about it – I'm by far the best athlete in this school!' _____

5 ★★★ **Choose three of the adjectives in the list. For each one, think of a person you know who can be described using that adjective. Write a short sentence to say why.**

> assertive | conceited | expressive | forceful
> impulsive | modest | self-assured | self-conscious

0 *My friend Sam is very impulsive. If he sees something he wants, he buys it right away.*

1 _____
_____

2 _____
_____

3 _____
_____

REFERENCE

body language
broken (French)
(can't) make (yourself) understood
communication breakdown
dialect
strong accent
facial expression
pronounce

Language and communication

first language
native speaker
follow
misunderstand
language barrier
interpret
incomprehensible
gesture

assertive
conceited
expressive

Personality (2)

forceful
self-conscious
self-assured
modest
impulsive

VOCABULARY EXTRA

1   Read the post and find six behaviour collocations.

Life lesson: no 245

Do you lose your patience with your parents when they joke about what you're wearing? Do you sometimes throw a tantrum like a toddler 😠 when they say you can't do something? Don't worry, it's perfectly normal! Try these top tips to help you communicate better with them.

- Try not to be so sensitive. If you can't take a joke, don't be mad at them.

- Come to terms with your relationship with them, don't fight it! Try to accept that they don't understand what it's like to be Gen Z. 🙂

- Don't fight it. Swallow your pride and say sorry. They'll appreciate that.

- You can reveal your true character to your friends. For the moment, just be who your parents want you to be. One day, they'll understand.

Try it and let me know.

2   Circle the correct verbs.

1   I've *throw* / *come* to terms with not getting a place on the language course.

2   Try not to *lose* / *swallow* your patience with him if he doesn't understand immediately.

3   It's good to show your emotions and *reveal* / *take* your true character so people can help you.

4   I think you'd better *swallow* / *lose* your pride and apologise to Eva for what you said.

5   What's wrong with you? Can't you *reveal* / *take* a joke?

6   My young nephew *comes* / *throws* a tantrum when he doesn't get what he wants.

3   Complete the sentences so they are true for you.

1   I sometimes lose my patience when
_____
_____

2   The last time I swallowed my pride was
_____
_____

3   This year I have had to come to terms with
_____
_____

THE MAN WHO SPEAKS
32 LANGUAGES

Inside a grey office building in Brussels, Ioannis Ikonomou's workload is marked in different colours on his computer screen. The 49-year-old Greek translator has received three special requests: The EU Commission urgently needs translations of confidential documents from Hebrew, Chinese and Azerbaijani. Very few of the EU's 2,500 translators can handle that. **A** ☐ He speaks 32 languages virtually fluently, including a pair of dead languages. What his brain has managed to achieve is perhaps unique on the planet. How can a human being learn so many languages? And how does he live with that?

Ikonomou regards questions like that as 'funny'. **B** ☐ He says his career developed out of curiosity. 'That's a keyword for my life.'

He learned English at age five, German at seven ('Frau Rosi, a German lady on Crete, taught me'), Italian when he was barely 10 ('a school friend started to take it, and I wanted to be better than he was'), Russian at 13 ('I loved Dostoyevsky'), East African Swahili at 14 ('just for fun') and Turkish at 16.

But it wasn't just his curiosity that turned Ikonomou into a language nut. **C** ☐ 'My friends all listened to the same Greek songs and ate souvlaki,' he says. 'But I wanted to get away from souvlaki, from my culture, from my roots. I was the opposite of Odysseus.' **D** ☐ 'The rules of a language are only the beginning for me,' he says.

'I want to understand everything — the food, the music, the religion, the traumas of a people.' Then he took a giant step: Ikonomou suddenly became fascinated by India, and studied Urdu, Hindi and Sanskrit. **E** ☐

Ikonomou speaks 21 of the total of 24 official EU languages. 'I forgot my Lithuanian, and I didn't have time for Gaelic or Maltese.' He understands not only modern languages, but also various old ones – Latin, of course, but also Old English, Mayan, Old Irish and Old Iranian.

'**F** ☐,' he says. 'When you really fall in love with someone you also want to know their whole story, meet their parents, visit their old schools. A language is not just the present for me but also the past.'

Ikonomou's work requires him to translate primarily official documents, but he listens to worldwide chats, internet TV, radio on his smartphone in the mornings and evenings on the way to and from work, always in different languages. Lately he's been keeping up with the news in Chinese.

'Chinese is my favourite language,' he says. 'It's completely different, the Mount Everest for Europeans.' He's been to China a few times. **G** ☐ The costs are borne by the Commission, mostly.

There are some countries whose languages he speaks that Ikonomou has never visited, including Ethiopia and the Congo. 'I just don't have the time', he says.

📖 READING

1 **Read the article quickly and find out …**

  1 where this man works, and who for.
    _____

  2 why he started learning languages. _____

  3 which languages he doesn't speak. _____

2 **Put the sentences into the correct spaces in the article. There is one sentence you do not need.**

  1 Nor was it his intelligence, which won him membership in the high-IQ society Mensa International. ☐

  2 Language is like love. ☐

  3 He didn't play football, and most school subjects bored him. ☐

  4 So Ikonomou kept up his travels through the languages and cultures of the world and continues to do so to this day. ☐

  5 Ikonomou is the best of them all. ☐

  6 With each visit, he learned more of the language. ☐

  7 He's never asked them of himself. ☐

  8 For 18 years, he was a strict vegetarian and lived by Hindu rules. ☐

3 **CRITICAL THINKING** **Which statements do you think Ioannis Ikonomou would agree with? Give reasons.**

  1 'It's easy to understand everything about a person from another country even if you can't speak their language.'

  2 'Learning a language is learning about a culture and its people.'

  3 'We don't need to learn other languages. Our own language is enough.'

  4 'A language is more than just words.'

4 **Write three questions that you would ask Ikonomou if you met him. Then write what you think his answers might be.**

  1 _____
    _____

  2 _____
    _____

  3 _____
    _____

DEVELOPING Writing

Writing up data from a graph

1 INPUT Read the survey results quickly. What was the purpose of the survey?

A school wanted to find out …

A why some courses were more popular than others.

B why people who contacted them about courses decided not to enrol.

C why some students decided to enrol there and not another school.

2 ANALYSE Look at the graph and read the results again. Answer the questions.

1 Number the reasons in the order in which the writer discusses them.

2 Which reasons does the writer make a comment about?

_____

3 Find an underlined word or expression in the text which means …

1 a result of _____

2 are the reason for _____

3 come to the conclusion _____

4 especially _____

5 interesting enough to mention _____

6 most important reason _____

7 so _____

8 together with _____

4 PLAN You are going to write up the results of another survey that the school undertook to find out why students enrolled for a second term. Look at the graph showing the results and answer the questions.

1 In which order do you think you will write about them?

2 Which ones are you going to explore in more detail? Number them in order and make brief notes.

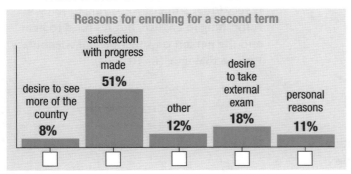

5 PRODUCE Write up the results (200–220 words). Use your answers from Exercise 4 and the structure below. Make your own checklist.

- Include an introduction.
- Discuss the reasons in the order you decided in Exercise 4.
- Use the survey results above to help you.
- Use as many of the expressions in Exercise 3 as you can.

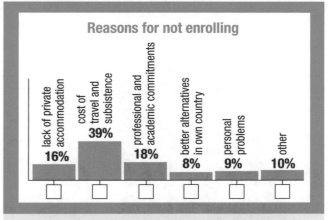

A school that offers courses in English decided to do a survey. They wanted to find out why people who contacted them about courses decided not to enrol.

Survey results

We conducted a survey of people who had contacted us about our courses but decided not to enrol. We wanted to find out more about the reasons for their decision. The results can be found in the bar chart above.

As can be seen, <u>the most significant factor</u> was how much it costs to travel to our country, <u>coupled with</u> the cost of living while they're here. Recent changes in exchange rates <u>account for</u> a lot of this concern, and <u>thus</u> we cannot necessarily <u>infer</u> that our fees are too high.

18% of respondents stated that a change to their work or college/university commitments meant that they were unable to take up the course they had hoped to enrol in.

One factor <u>worth noting</u> is that the decision of 16% of respondents not to enrol with us is <u>down to</u> the fact that we can only offer accommodation with local families – adult customers <u>in particular</u> stated that they wished to have private accommodation of some kind.

Other motives for not enrolling include personal problems (e.g. illness), as well as the discovery of alternative courses in the respondent's own country which they felt were at least as suitable, if not more so.

Finally, 10% of respondents selected 'other reasons', but none of them stated what those reasons were.

✓ CHECKLIST

☐ _____

☐ _____

🎧 LISTENING

1 🔊 **8.01** **Listen to a podcast. What is it about?**

A The boroughs of
New York City ☐

B The different
languages spoken
in New York City ☐

C The best ways to travel to each borough
in New York City ☐

2 🔊 **8.01** **Listen again. Complete the sentences with a
word or short phrase.**

1 There are more than ¹_____ languages
spoken within a 16-kilometre radius of New York City.

2 There are only one or two ²_____ of
Gottscheerisch.

3 Some older members of Croatian families
³_____ when they arrived in
New York City.

4 A speaker of Mandaic is creating a dictionary to help future
speakers ⁴_____ and understand how it
works.

5 One refugee is aware that a person's native language is a big
part of ⁵_____ . A written list is being
produced to help students de-code the grammar, definitions
and pronunciation of their tribal language.

6 Garifuna originated in Honduras and Belize, but it is
⁶_____ it is where it originated.

7 Students who are learning Garifuna through music are also
learning about their culture and ⁷_____ .

DIALOGUE

1 **Complete the dialogues with the words and
phrases in the list.**

> didn't catch | didn't get | don't follow
> don't see | familiar with | lost me

1 **A** It's very noisy in here, isn't it?
  B What? Sorry – I
    _____ that. Can you
    say it again?

2 **A** So, I decided not to do any more work on
    it, it was a thankless task.
  B 'Thankless task'? I'm not
    _____ that
    expression. Could you explain, please?

3 **A** So, in cricket, when a player is out, he
    goes back in and another player comes
    out to go in.
  B I'm sorry, you've
    _____ completely.
    What does that all mean?

4 **A** I'm sorry but I just
    _____ your argument
    at all.
  B OK, let me try to explain it another way.

5 **A** It's an interesting idea, but hard to
    understand.
  B That's right. To be honest, I
    _____ what he
    means at all.

6 **A** Wasn't that a great joke that she told?
  B Well, to be honest, I
    _____ it. That's why I
    didn't laugh much.

2 **Imagine you are at a party where the music
is very loud. Someone is trying to tell you
something in English, but it's hard to hear
and the person is using unusual vocabulary.
Write a dialogue (8–10 lines).**

_____
_____
_____
_____
_____
_____
_____
_____
_____
_____
_____

> **PRONUNCIATION**
> Stress in multi-syllable words
> Go to page 120. 🎧

C1 Advanced

1 **You are going to read four film reviews. For questions 1–4, choose from the reviews A–D. The reviews may be chosen more than once.**

REVIEWER A

This film features the wartime story of how Native Americans worked as radio operators using a code based on the Navajo language, and the efforts of soldiers to protect both them and the code. It's a good storyline, and the film has amusing moments and some good action scenes, so it is enjoyable to watch, but it's mostly unrealistic fantasy. The director obviously hasn't done much research into either the realities of war, or the equipment used. For example, Nicolas Cage, who plays the lead character, uses a different kind of gun every time he's on screen, and often one quite unsuited to the situation. It's also incredible that the constant noise of war ceases the moment Cage needs to talk to one of his buddies. Unfortunately, all this does is draw attention to their rather unconvincing exchanges. Cage is a good actor, whose other work has been impressive, but he doesn't really get to grips with this part.

REVIEWER B

Although it's fun to watch, and moves along at quite a pace with plenty of action, this has to be one of the least well researched war films there has ever been. Anyone familiar with US army uniforms will soon spot the inconsistencies here. Nicolas Cage is sometimes excellent in films but this is a big miss for him, in my opinion. However, he's far less culpable than the director who seems to have taken great liberties with the original story of the Navajo code that the film is supposedly centred around. I say 'supposedly' because if you don't know much about the code-talkers (as they were called), you'll leave this film not much the wiser. But there are some nice moments in the film, and the scriptwriters have done a great job in recreating plausible interaction between the soldiers, so it's certainly worth watching.

REVIEWER C

This director has made several other war films. Usually there's a strong mix of action and character portrayal. Here though, the characters definitely take second place, and that's a shame. What should've been an interesting story didn't hold my attention and I quickly lost interest in the action scenes. Although the everyday details of army life seem to be quite well reproduced, there is some very inauthentic sounding dialogue, and other aspects of the film appear to be made up. There is little evidence that the Navajo code-talkers ever received 'protection', so the central storyline is pure fantasy – and there simply isn't enough on which to construct a drama that will make us care about the main characters. You can't fault Nicolas Cage or the rest of the cast, who do their best to bring the story to life, but over-the-top direction cancels out their efforts.

REVIEWER D

In this war drama with a twist, Nicolas Cage plays a war-weary soldier who has to take a young Navajo recruit under his wing. Even if you're a fan of Cage, you'll have to admit that it hardly ranks amongst his best ever performances and it may be because the cast are rather let down by the quality of the screenwriting – the way the two central characters speak to each other just didn't convince this viewer I'm afraid. The story centres around a code developed using the Navajo language that needs to be kept out of enemy hands. Quite a lot of effort seems to have gone into recreating the backdrop of the military setting, with great attention paid to getting every aspect of the uniforms and equipment right, but the actual plot line didn't grip me and I came away feeling rather underwhelmed and disappointed.

Which reviewer …

1 makes a similar overall assessment of the entertainment value of the film to Reviewer D? ☐

2 has the same opinion as Reviewer C regarding the accuracy of the details in the film. ☐

3 has a different view to the others regarding the performance of the main actor? ☐

4 has a different view to Reviewer A regarding the naturalness of the dialogue? ☐

CONSOLIDATION

🎧 LISTENING

1 🔊 **8.03** **Listen to the conversation between Gina and Steve. What is Steve wearing under his suit jacket?**

2 🔊 **8.03** **Listen again and answer the questions.**

1 What is Steve wearing on his feet?
_____

2 Why does Gina object to them?
_____

3 What does Gina recommend he wears?
_____

4 Why will it be hard to find photos of Gina wearing bad fashion?
_____

5 What did Gina use to do with loom bands?
_____

6 What other item did Gina use to wear that she now regrets?
_____

7 What's her biggest piece of fashion advice?
_____

Ⓖ GRAMMAR

3 **Match the sentences.**

1 Another piece of cake? ☐
2 Do you think we can win? ☐
3 I don't think we've got enough time to walk to the station. ☐
4 Whatever you do, don't tell Ian. ☐
5 Got any chocolate? ☐
6 You used to do yoga. ☐
7 However hard I try, I just can't do it. ☐
8 Lucy's got over 500 friends on Facebook. ☐

a Certainly hope so.
b Yes, most of whom she wouldn't recognise if she met them in the street.
c Why not? Is it a secret?
d Still do.
e Love one.
f Don't give up now.
g In which case let's get a taxi.
h Yes, want some?

4 **Complete the sentences with a phrase from the list.**

> both of whom | neither of them | whenever
> however | none of which | whoever

1 _____ wrote these homework questions is very cruel.
2 There are 12 questions, _____ I have the slightest idea about.
3 _____ hard I try, I just can't make any sense of them.
4 My mind just goes blank _____ I look at them.
5 I've asked my brothers, _____ think they're good at Maths, for help.
6 _____ could help me.

🔤 VOCABULARY

5 **Complete the missing words.**

1 His interest in cars was very s_____-l_____ and quickly replaced by football.
2 When I hear my five-year-old singing in the school play it brings a t_____ to my e_____ .
3 She's quite s_____-c_____ and awkward around people she doesn't know very well.
4 From her b_____ l_____ I would say she's not very impressed by you at all.
5 He speaks French well but his s_____ English a_____ can make him difficult to understand.
6 His speech was incredibly moving. It sent s_____ down my s_____ .
7 This new smart phone really is a m_____-h_____ and everyone will be wanting one soon.
8 She's very s_____-a_____ and confident in all she does.

6 **Choose the correct options.**

1 She's a brilliant pianist, but you'd never know because she's so *modest / conceited / expressive*.
2 We are cousins, but there's a bit of a language *wall / barrier / fence* between us. Juan's English isn't perfect and my Spanish is virtually non-existent.
3 Jeans never really go *off / out of / in to* fashion.
4 The water was so cold it gave me *duck / goose / swan* bumps everywhere.
5 The holiday was great and I just about got by with my *broken / wrecked / damaged* French.
6 She just goes with however she's feeling in the moment. She's very *assertive / forceful / impulsive*.
7 I love this song. It makes my *head / heart / lungs* soar every time I hear it.
8 Beards are really *all / in / it* at the moment. It seems that lots of men have got one these days.

DIALOGUE

7 **Put the dialogue in order.**

[ ] **Shop assistant** It leaves your hair shiny and healthy. It's good for your hair and the environment. I think everyone should take a bit more care of the environment.

[ ] **Shop assistant** OK, I'll be quick. Imagine using a product on your hair that doesn't damage the environment.

[1] **Shop assistant** Excuse me. Can I introduce you to our new eco-friendly hair products?

[ ] **Shop assistant** I said, can I introduce you to our new eco-friendly hair products.

[ ] **Shop assistant** In that case, using a product like Green Hair means you won't need to think about it ever again.

[ ] **Freya** So do I. OK. I'll try it!

[ ] **Freya** I've never thought about the hair products I use like that.

[2] **Freya** Sorry, I didn't catch what you said with all the noise.

[ ] **Freya** So, why should I buy this and not my usual brand?

[ ] **Freya** OK but be quick, I'm a bit short of time.

READING

8 **Read the article. Complete facts 1–9 with the words in the list. Can you think of the answers to the final fact?**

bookkeeper | euouae | feedback | ough | pangram | purple | rhythm | uncopyrightable | unprosperousness

AMAZE YOUR FRIENDS WITH ...

10 INCREDIBLE FACTS ABOUT THE ENGLISH LANGUAGE!

[1]_____ means the state of not being wealthy or profitable. It's not the easiest word to use or remember, but it is the longest word in English in which each letter is used at least two times.

[2]_____ is that horrible noise you get when your microphone is too close to the speaker. It is also the shortest word in English that contains the first six letters of the alphabet.

There are no words in English that rhyme with 'month,' 'orange,' 'silver,' or [3]_____ , so don't try using them in a poem (that is if you want it to rhyme).

A [4]_____ is someone who counts the money and does the accounts. It is also the only English word that has three consecutive double letters.

[5]_____ is used to describe something such as a photo or a piece of writing that no one has permission to use. More memorably, perhaps, it is the longest English word that contains no letter more than once.

Vowels (a, e, i, o and u) might be the most useful letters in the language. After all, it's pretty difficult to write anything without using one. There is one word, however, you can make: [6]_____ .

And at the other extreme, [7]_____ is the longest word in English that contains only vowels. It's a medieval music term but don't ask us exactly what it means or how to pronounce it. Admittedly it's not the most useful word.

The letter combination [8]_____ has nine different ways that it can be pronounced. You'll find them all in the following sentence: 'A rough-coated, dough-faced, thoughtful ploughman strode through the streets of Scarborough; after falling into a slough, he coughed and hiccoughed.' Good luck saying that!

A [9]_____ is a sentence that contains all 26 letters of the alphabet. The most famous example of this is: 'The quick brown fox jumps over the lazy dog.'

And finally, only two English words end in '-gry'. Can you think what they are?

WRITING

9 **Research and write down five amazing facts about your first language.**

9 FAIRNESS MATTERS

Grammar video

▶ 23

GRAMMAR
Negative inversion

→ SB p.86

1 ★☆☆ **Circle the correct options.**

Timeless memories

1 *Never / Little* had Marianne been happier than she was on her wedding day.
2 *Little / Rarely* has a romance been more intense.
3 *Not only / On no account* was Dominic a famous photographer, but he was her dream partner as well.
4 *No sooner / Not only* had they arrived at their hotel than the sun came up.
5 *Little / Never* had they seen a more beautiful dawn.
6 *No sooner / Not only* was the sky wonderful, but the lake sparkled beautifully, too.
7 *Rarely / On no account* do we have the opportunity to photograph something as lovely as that.
8 *Rarely / Under no circumstances* would Marianne let Dominic sell the photos of their trip.
9 *On no account / Not only* could anyone see or publish these photos.
10 *Little / Never* did she know how valuable they would become.

2 ★★☆ **Complete the sentences with a correct form of the verbs in brackets.**

1 Never _____ they _____ a more exciting match than the one on TV last night. (see)
2 On no account _____ Jack _____ to the top of the tower. He's afraid of heights. (climb)
3 No sooner _____ the clock _____ midnight than the spell was broken and Cinderella had to run out of the ballroom. (strike)
4 Rarely _____ we _____ the chance to hear such beautiful music in a shopping centre! (have)
5 Not only _____ the room in the hotel dirty, but the breakfast was awful, too. (be)
6 Never again _____ the river _____ over, because the world is getting warmer. (freeze)
7 Under no circumstances _____ the shop _____ the money because Jane has worn the skirt. (return)
8 Only once every few years _____ Mario _____ his grandparents in South America. (visit)

3 ★★☆ **Rewrite the sentences starting with the word in brackets.**

1 I have never been so shocked by a programme shown on TV. (Never)
_____

2 It was untrue, and wildly exaggerated, too. (Not only ... but)
_____

3 I don't usually complain about TV programmes. (Rarely)
_____

4 I phoned the TV company immediately after the programme finished. (No sooner ... than)
_____

5 The person I spoke to was rude and he seemed to think my complaint was funny. (Not only ... but)
_____

6 I had no idea the programme was meant to be a comedy. (Little)
_____

4 ★★★ **There are six sentences in this paragraph which can be changed into negative inversions. Find them and rewrite them using *under no circumstances*, *never*, *not only ... but*, *little* and *rarely*.**

Jeb had his dream job working in the garage of a racing team. He worked on the cars and was also allowed to drive them on the test track. The track was designed to test racing cars, but the boss told Jeb that he could never go faster than 100 kph. But Jeb was happy just to be in the cars. He had never enjoyed a job so much. Last Tuesday, he was taking a car round the track for a final test. Just as he turned the last bend the car slid off the track and crashed into the wall. The boss was furious. 'I don't often see such bad driving from my staff!' he yelled, 'I'll never let you drive again.' But he didn't know that there was oil on the track. When he found out, he apologised to Jeb and said he understood it wasn't his fault and that of course Jeb could continue to drive the cars.

Spoken discourse markers → SB p.89

5 ★☆☆ **Circle the correct options.**

One person's thoughts about hunting wild animals

1 *To be honest / Let's face it*, I've never been on a hunting trip and I don't want to go.

2 *Personally / If you ask me*, we've done enough harm to wild animals without hunting them.

3 *On the other hand / By the way*, there might be good reasons for reducing the number of some animals in over-populated areas.

4 *Personally / Mind you*, it'd be a huge responsibility to decide which animals should be killed.

5 *To tell you the truth / However*, there are more humane ways of doing that than hunting.

6 *Let's face it / Because of*, amateur hunters may not always be very good at shooting.

7 *By the way / The thing is*, it's just a matter of who has the money to pay to hunt, you don't have to prove you can shoot.

8 I'm surprised people haven't found an answer yet. *That said / For a start*, it's not an easy problem to solve.

6 ★★★ **Five of the underlined discourse markers in this dialogue are incorrect. Find and correct them. Sometimes there is more than one answer.**

Will Andi, do you think it's OK to do what you like with money?

Andi Yeah. [1]For a start, if it's my money, why not?

Will [2]The thing is, I've been reading this book and it raises some interesting questions.

Andi Like what?

Will [3]Nevertheless, is it OK for someone to jump to the front of the queue just because they paid more?

Andi [4]Personally, I think that's OK at an airport or somewhere. [5]On the other hand, using your time instead of your money is your choice. [6]As a result, perhaps it's different in somewhere like a hospital. I don't think people should get special treatment because they can pay more. That's not fair.

Will [7]To be honest, I can't see the difference. You're using money to buy privilege.

Andi I suppose so. [8]While I'd do it if I could.

Will [9]Actually, I don't know what to think.

Andi Well, [10]at the end of the day, we have to make choices all the time. Don't worry about it. [11]For a start, did you finish that history project?

Will Huh? Oh yes, the history project …

7 ★★★ **Write a short dialogue for two of these situations. Include the discourse markers in the list and any others that are appropriate.**

> because of | however | if you ask me
> let's face it | that said | to be honest
> to tell you the truth | while

1 Vanessa and Seb are talking about a film they watched last night. Vanessa enjoyed it, but Seb didn't.

2 Milo and Jane are discussing the test they've just finished. Milo thinks it was easy, Jane doesn't.

3 Karl and Helena are talking about the new restaurant that has opened in the town.

GET IT RIGHT!

Discourse markers

When using discourse markers, learners often position them incorrectly in the sentence.

✓ *Personally, I don't believe that he's right.*

✗ *I don't believe ~~personally~~ that he's right.*

Identify and underline the discourse marker in each sentence. Then tick (✓) the sentences which are correct. Rewrite the incorrect ones.

0 I was convinced that the suspect, <u>to be honest</u>, had committed the crime.

To be honest, I was convinced that the suspect had committed the crime.

1 Let's face it, drugs testing on animals is unethical.

_____ ☐

2 I do believe Kate was treated unfairly. She should have studied harder, that said.

_____ ☐

3 There seems to be a lot in the news about corrupt politicians at the moment. There are lots of other corrupt people mind you, too!

_____ ☐

4 The thing is, a lot of people are prejudiced and it's difficult to overcome this.

_____ ☐

5 It isn't really justifiable to spend so much money on prisons when there are so many other important things at the end of the day.

_____ ☐

VOCABULARY
Court cases

→ SB p.86

1 ★☆☆ Complete the crossword.

1 A doctor gave _____ that the accused man was mentally ill.

2 She made a _____ to the police and said she had committed the crime.

3 The prosecution is not allowed to _____ evidence from the defence lawyers.

4 The judge said he was _____ and sent him to prison.

5 There was a _____ who said he had seen the crime happen.

6 The judge said she was _____ and she was free to go home.

7 If you think the verdict is wrong, you can _____ .

8 He said that his confession wasn't true and he wanted to _____ it.

9 In our country, if you murder someone you get sentenced to _____ imprisonment.

10 There is a lawyer for the prosecution, and one for the _____ .

2 ★★☆ Circle the correct options.

A I saw the crime and I am certain that Mr Wright is not the man I saw running out of the shop. I believe that Mr Wright is ¹*innocent / guilty*. So I am going to give ²*evidence / confession* in the court case – I will be a ³*lawyer / witness* for the ⁴*defence / prosecution* and I hope Mr Wright will go home a free man.

B When she was arrested, Mrs Ashton made ⁵*an appeal / a confession* but later she said that she wanted to ⁶*give / retract* what she had said before. She said that the police had ⁷*given / withheld* evidence that would show she was innocent. However, the jury did not believe her and ⁸*found / made* her guilty. Mrs Ashton was given a sentence of ten years' ⁹*prosecution / imprisonment*.

Fairness and equality

→ SB p.89

3 ★★☆ Complete the sentences with the words in the list.

> equal | evident | general | obese
> political | social | unfair | violent

1 Most schools do not face a serious threat from _____ crime.

2 Being _____ can be related to poverty.

3 _____ problems like loneliness and bad health are increasing in certain parts of the country.

4 It is _____ that more crimes are committed by males than females.

5 In _____ , all parents want the best for their children.

6 An _____ society is something we would like to see in the future.

7 The new president will make _____ changes to help everyone in the town.

8 I think the new law on pay is _____ . Women and men deserve the same.

WordWise:
Expressions with on

→ SB p.87

4 ★★☆ Match the replies with the dialogues. Then complete the replies with the words in the list.

> basis | behalf | terms | trial | way

1 **A** Why can't I ask you these questions?
  B ☐

2 **A** How's she getting on with the piano?
  B ☐

3 **A** The police have arrested Marco!
  B ☐

4 **A** I hear Alice can't come to the meeting.
  B ☐

5 **A** So, your mother knows the head of the school?
  B ☐

a Because I feel like I'm on _____ for something!

b Yes, they're on pretty friendly _____ with each other.

c That's right, so she's asked me to talk on her _____ .

d Really well! She's on her _____ to being a very good player.

e I know, but I don't understand on what _____ he's being accused.

REFERENCE

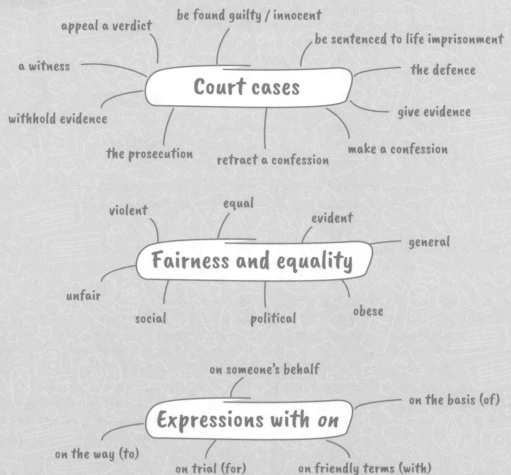

Court cases

- appeal a verdict
- be found guilty / innocent
- a witness
- be sentenced to life imprisonment
- the defence
- withhold evidence
- give evidence
- make a confession
- the prosecution
- retract a confession

Fairness and equality

- violent
- equal
- evident
- general
- unfair
- social
- political
- obese

Expressions with on

- on someone's behalf
- on the basis (of)
- on the way (to)
- on trial (for)
- on friendly terms (with)

VOCABULARY EXTRA

1 Match the words to make collocations related to punishments.

1	have a fair	a	on trial
2	carry out	b	a (heavy) fine
3	go	c	a verdict
4	face	d	in court
5	reach	e	trial
6	appear	f	an investigation

2 Complete the newspaper article with collocations from Exercise 1.

3 Write your own definitions for each collocation in Exercise 1.

1 _____
2 _____
3 _____
4 _____
5 _____
6 _____

Police will ¹_____ into the financial affairs of a local company. If the two company owners are guilty, they are likely to ²_____ for fraud and tax evasion. If the company owners eventually ³_____ as a result of the investigation and the jury ⁴_____ of guilty, the owners will be likely to ⁵_____ of up to €10,000, but not prison sentences. In order for the two owners to ⁶_____ , newspapers cannot reveal the names of the people involved.

One thing that seems to be a feature of all human beings is a notion of fairness – but what does it really mean? Most people would agree that it means thinking about the needs and interests of other people when making decisions about how to behave and striking a balance between our needs and theirs. OK, but does everyone share the same idea of what's fair and what isn't? Clearly not! There's a lot of variation between individual people and between cultures – some people tend to be more selfish, inconsiderate and colder than others. Yet if you ask people 'Are you a fair person?' almost everyone will answer 'Yes,' won't they? Let's face it, not many people are willing to put up their hands and say, 'I don't think I'm a fair person,' or, 'the world isn't fair, so neither am I'!

So, what about you – are you a fair person? I've put together a 'quiz' – some questions for you to answer with either 'Yes' or 'No' to see how fair you really are. How would you answer these questions?

1 A mother and father have two children – one aged 15, one aged 9. They give the same monthly pocket money to each child. Is this fair?

2 Someone lends you a book, and accidentally you tear the corner of one of the pages. You tell this to the person who lent you the book – the person asks you to buy them a new book. Is this fair?

3 You are standing in a queue to get some coffee in a coffee shop. Someone runs past everyone in the queue, saying 'Sorry, I'm really late!' and goes to the front of the queue. Is this fair?

4 A student has to write an essay for school. Another student offers to write the paper for them, for £50. The first student accepts, pays and gets top marks. Is this fair?

5 The electricity workers are on strike and homes have no electricity, so people have to use battery-powered torches. Some shopkeepers increase the price of their torches and batteries. Is this fair?

6 There is a school in a town that has the best facilities and the best teachers, but they only accept students whose parents have enough money to pay the school fees. Is this fair?

Of course, this quiz can't possibly tell us if you treat people fairly or not in real life, can it? So, what's the point? Well, it shows us that in every one of the six situations there are two sides to every story and that we should always try to see the other person's point of view, even if we think there is only one correct answer.

📖 READING

1 Read the blog. Choose the best title.

   A Are you as fair as you think you are?

   B Why fairness matters to people

   C How different people define 'fairness'

2 Read the blog again and answer the questions.

   1 What two things need to be balanced for something to be fair?

   _____

   2 What are many people not willing to do?

   _____

   3 What did the writer try to do when compiling the quiz?

   _____

   4 Which of the situations concerns damage to property?

   _____

   5 Which situation has nothing to do with money?

   _____

   6 What was the writer's real purpose in compiling the quiz?

   _____

3 CRITICAL THINKING Read about the situation and the responses (A–C). Which response(s) is/are fair, in your opinion?

Situation: You borrow a friend's laptop, but you drop it and the screen is smashed. You apologise to your friend and offer to pay for the repair.

Your friend:

   A says you must buy them a new laptop.

   B thanks you and says paying half will be enough.

   C tells you not to worry. Their parents are willing to pay for the repair.

4 Write the dialogue (8–10 lines) between the two friends in Exercise 3.

> **PRONUNCIATION**
> *Unstressed syllables and words: the /ɪ/ phoneme.*
> Go to page 120.

DEVELOPING ✎ *Writing*

Writing an essay

THE PUNISHMENT SHOULD FIT THE CRIME – AND THE CRIMINAL.

Some people believe that for each type of criminal <u>offence</u>, the person responsible should receive the same punishment, no matter what the circumstances. ¹_____ , I believe that the system which we have in place now in the UK, whereby judges can <u>use their discretion</u> when sentencing someone, is far better.

Let us take an example. ²_____ that the fixed sentence for shoplifting is a three-month jail sentence. This means that every person caught shoplifting would go to prison for three months, no matter who the person is (or what they stole). ³_____ , it is not at all difficult to see that such a situation would be unfair. Once we begin to consider differences between people, like their age or their personal circumstances, it becomes clear that a judge needs to be able to choose from within a range of possible sentences.

Should a 17-year-old unemployed person, convicted of shoplifting for the first time, be given the same sentence as a 40-year-old employed person who has been <u>convicted</u> several times before? I do not believe so. ⁴_____ , I would argue that it would be completely wrong to give the 17-year-old <u>first-time offender</u> a prison sentence: that would be far too <u>severe</u> and it would also put them into contact with other criminals. Something more <u>lenient</u> would be more appropriate – for example, <u>community service</u> and a suspended sentence. ⁵_____ , someone who has offended many times should go to prison for more than just three months.

⁶_____ , it is my opinion that judges should have a range of sentencing options available to them for most offences, which allows them <u>to take into account</u> the circumstances both of the crime and of the person involved.

---

1 [INPUT] **Read the essay and choose the correct options.**

1 The essay is mainly about …
- **A** the need to make punishments for certain crimes more severe.
- **B** not punishing unemployed people.
- **C** adjusting punishments according to who committed the crime.

2 The writer believes that judges …
- **A** are too strict when they sentence people.
- **B** should choose from a range of punishments.
- **C** should punish 40-year-old people more strictly than 17-year-old people.

2 [ANALYSE] **Complete the essay with the words in the list.**

> arguably | consequently | however
> imagine | in fact | now

3 **Match the underlined words and phrases in the essay with the definitions (1–8).**

1 an action which is against the law _____

2 someone who had not committed a crime before _____

3 found guilty in a court of law _____

4 work that is to help other people, and is done without payment (sometimes as a punishment) _____

5 not kind or showing sympathy _____

6 to consider or remember something when judging a situation _____

7 use their right or ability to decide something _____

8 not a strong type of punishment _____

4 [PLAN] **You are going to write an essay titled 'Shaming offenders'. Make notes on the positive and negative points of this idea.**

> Sometimes a judge might decide to 'shame' someone as punishment for a crime they've committed. For example, a shoplifter might be sent back to the shop to stand outside with a sign that says: 'I stole from this shop.'

5 [PRODUCE] **Write your essay (250–300 words). Use your notes from Exercise 4 and the ideas below. Write your own checklist.**
- do some internet research for examples of 'shaming'
- state what shaming consists of
- say what your overall opinion is
- give examples of how this is a positive or negative idea

✓ CHECKLIST
- ☐ _____
- ☐ _____
- ☐ _____
- ☐ _____
- ☐ _____

 LISTENING

1 🔊 9.02 **Listen to Maisie and Jake talking about a film. Tick (✓) the statement below which is NOT true.**

a ☐ The film is about three American mathematicians and engineers.

b ☐ It's about three women who struggle with equality and fairness.

c ☐ The women lose their jobs when computers are introduced in their workplace.

2 🔊 9.02 **Listen again. Answer the questions.**

1 When is the film set? _____

2 What does NASA stand for? _____

3 What was the problem for the main characters at the start of their careers?
_____

4 What were the segregation rules in Virginia at that time?
_____

5 What does Maisie tell Jake about the women's male colleagues?
_____

6 What does Maisie say about equality for women today?
_____

DIALOGUE

1 **Put the dialogues in the correct order.**

1
	Mo	No, it doesn't. And more to the point, that's six years of his life that he'll never get back. He's in his mid-50s now.
1	Mo	Did you hear about that man who got released from prison?
	Mo	I'm not sure, but I'd have thought it won't be easy for him to restart his life.
	Mo	Or even longer. It can be hard for people who've left prison to find a job.
	Mo	Something like six years, if I'm not mistaken. And for something he didn't do!
	Sam	Wow, that's a long time. It really doesn't seem fair, does it?
	Sam	Well, I heard something, yes. How long had he been in prison?
	Sam	You're right, it'll take around a couple of months, I think.
	Sam	Well, when you put it like that, it sounds even worse. Poor guy. What do you think he'll do now?

2
	Alana	Really? So, how much is too much?
	Alana	OK, sorry. Well, it's a shame you can't come. Maybe next month?
1	Alana	Do you want to come out tonight? I'm meeting up with Jack and the others.
	Alana	That doesn't seem fair. Why on earth have they done that?
	Alana	Well when you put it like that, I can see what your parents mean.
	Leah	Hey, you're supposed to be my best friend – don't take my parents' side!
	Leah	Well, I'd like to, but I can't. My parents have told me I can only go out twice a month.
	Leah	Well, one evening last month I spent in the region of £50, give or take. It was just under my whole allowance for the month.
	Leah	Oh, they say I've got to do more studying. And more to the point, they reckon I spend too much.

PHRASES FOR FLUENCY

→ SB p.90

1 **Complete the phrases with the missing words.**

0 ___apparently___

1 I'd _____ thought

2 more _____ point

3 it's _____ me

4 if _____ not
_____

5 _____ you
_____ it
_____ that

2 **Use a word or phrase from Exercise 1 to complete the dialogues.**

1 **A** This is a cool song. Who's the singer?
B Good question. I think it's Adele, _____ .

2 **A** Did you know she's a really good chess player?
B No, _____ .

3 **A** What happened to Leon? I heard he's in hospital.
B That's right. _____ he fell over and broke his arm.

4 **A** I don't like the colour of that shirt.
B Oh? That's strange. _____ it would be something you'd like.

5 **A** I think it was the worst film I've ever seen.
B Really? Well, _____ , maybe I won't go and see it.

6 **A** Why didn't you buy it?
B It was a bit expensive and _____ , I wasn't 100 percent sure I liked it.

C1 Advanced

🎧 LISTENING
Part 2: Sentence completion

1   🔊 9.03   You will hear a student called Monica Greaves giving a presentation about a month's work experience she did in a supermarket. For questions 1–8, complete the sentences with a word or short phrase.

🛒 WORK EXPERIENCE: SUPERMARKET

Monica's role at the supermarket involved what's called **(1)** _____ staff at various levels.

Monica was impressed by how **(2)** _____ the staff seemed to be.

Monica was surprised by the number of **(3)** _____ there were amongst the early morning shoppers.

In her first week, Monica worked with staff responsible for dealing with **(4)** _____ at the supermarket .

Monica uses the word **(5)** _____ to sum up her overall impression of the work she did in her second week.

Monica was surprised to see how much managers relied on **(6)** _____ when making decisions about ordering stock.

Monica was disappointed not to spend time in the supermarket's **(7)** _____ department.

Monica was pleased not to have to deal with too many **(8)** _____ in her final week.

✏️ WRITING
Part 2: a report

2   Write an answer to the question. Write your answer in 220–260 words in an appropriate style.

On a visit to an English-speaking country, you spent a month taking part in a work experience scheme. The company that organised the trip has asked you to write a report about the scheme.

In your report, you should explain: the type of work you did, what you gained from the experience and any advice you have for anyone thinking of taking part in the scheme in future.

Write your **report**.

GRAMMAR
Reported verb patterns (review)

→ SB p.94

1 ★☆☆ **Complete the phrases with the correct preposition.**

1 apologise _____ doing something
2 promise _____ do something
3 blame someone _____ doing something
4 decide _____ do something
5 insist _____ doing something
6 convince (someone) not _____ do something

2 ★★☆ **Complete the sentences with the correct form of the verbs.**

1 I recommend _____ (study) civil engineering at university.
2 My dad suggested _____ (take) a gap year.
3 My sister regrets _____ (not go) to university.
4 My brother has decided _____ (apply) to do a degree at Bath University.
5 I blamed myself for _____ (not pass) my English Literature A-Level.
6 York University has invited me _____ (speak) at a conference in March.

3 ★★☆ **Rewrite the sentences using reported verb patterns.**

0 'You passed! Well done,' Sam congratulated me.
Sam congratulated me on passing.

1 'You need to work harder,' warned Ms Gibbs.
_____

2 'You must go straight to university,' my parents insisted.
_____

3 'I've made a mistake,' admitted Jasper.
_____

4 'You could apply for a job instead of applying for university,' my headteacher suggested.
_____

4 ★★☆ **Complete the news story with the correct form of the verbs.**

In 2015, a British exam board promised
[1]_____ (change) their A-level music syllabus after a London teenager, Jesse McCabe, won her campaign to ensure female composers were studied on the course. The exam board apologised
[2]_____ (not feature) a single woman amongst the 63 composers. The board decided
[3]_____ (ask) leading academics who they felt should be included. Several of them suggested
[4]_____ (include) the 19th century German musician Clara Schumann and 17th century Italian Baroque singer Barbara Strozzi. The board also agreed [5]_____ (review) their other qualifications to ensure they were diverse and inclusive. The Managing Director personally apologised to the 17-year-old student
[6]_____ (not include) women on their A-Level syllabus. Other examining boards were also warned [7]_____ (review) their syllabuses. Many academics regretted
[8]_____ (not make) changes to their syllabuses earlier.

5 ★★★ **Use the prompts to complete the dialogue. Use the correct verb patterns.**

A I heard that your bike got stolen. Then you saw it up for sale on an online website. What did you do?
B [1]My friends / recommend / tell / the police
_____

A That sounds sensible to me. Then what did you do?
B [2]The police / warn / me / not / contact / the thief
_____

Then the police went to the thief's house.
A And what happened when they got to the house?
B [3]The police / accuse / man / steal / bike
_____

[4]He / confess / steal / it
_____

[5]He / apologise / take / it
_____

[6]And / he / promise / never / steal / anything / again
_____

Passive report structures
→ SB p.97

6 ★★☆ **Complete the theories about the benefits of studying certain subjects with a passive report structure. Use the verbs in brackets.**

1 Subjects such as Art, Music and Foreign Languages _____ have long-lasting benefits. (say)

2 Visual thinking _____ help children learn other subjects. (know)

3 Children who learn a musical instrument as a child _____ be able to listen and communicate better as adults. (believe)

4 It _____ children and adults who play a musical instrument for 30 minutes a week over the course of a year will have more highly developed brains. (think)

5 Exercise _____ extremely important for the cognitive development of children's brains. (consider)

7 ★★☆ **Rewrite the sentences using passive report structures.**

1 New research has found that 59 percent of UK graduates would choose a positive workplace over a better salary. (find)
It _____
_____
_____

2 In the UK in 2020, 60 percent of 2018/2019 graduates were working in a job that didn't require a degree. (report)
It _____
_____
_____

3 Research has established that in 2020, only 55 percent of 2018/2019 graduates were working in their chosen field. (establish)
It _____
_____
_____

4 A recruitment agency warned companies that if they failed to create career development programmes, they would miss the opportunity of attracting top talent. (warn)
Companies _____
_____
_____

5 By 2020, only 58 percent of 2018/2019 graduates had found secure full-time work. (confirm)
It _____
_____
_____

Hedging
→ SB p.97

8 ★★☆ **Rewrite the sentences with the 'vague' language in the list. Use each expression only once.**

> It is believed that | ~~might~~ | probably won't
> said to | seems to | thought that

0 Fruit lowers the risk of cancer.
Fruit might lower the risk of cancer.

1 It has been proved that eating pomegranates can strengthen your bones.
It is _____ .

2 Eating garlic will prevent you from catching a cold.
You _____ if you eat garlic.

3 Your memory will improve if you include blueberries in your diet.
Adding blueberries to your diet is
_____ .

4 Drinking green tea will help you lose weight.
Drinking green tea _____ .

5 Eating oily fish two or three times a week will protect your eyesight in old age.
_____ .

GET IT RIGHT!

Passive report structures

Learners often make mistakes when using passive report structures.

✓ *Beethoven is believed to have composed his first piece of music when he was three.*

✗ *Beethoven is believed to compose his first piece of music when he was three.*

Rewrite the sentences, making the underlined words the subject of each sentence.

1 It is reported that the government has plans to make cuts to the education budget.
_____

2 It was thought at one time that the world was flat.
_____

3 It is known that having a gap year can be beneficial to character development.
_____

4 It was found that the dissertation had been plagiarised.
_____

5 It is said that the family next door won the lottery last year.
_____

6 It is reported that the US president is going to visit the UK.
_____

VOCABULARY
Higher education

→ SB p.94

1 ★★☆ **Unscramble the words in brackets to complete the dialogue.**

Ella Well, you finally finished writing that
¹_____ (sserditatnio), and you
²_____ (adslie) through your final exams.
Well done! So, what are you going to do now?

Finn I'm hoping to do a ³_____ (saMret's)
degree next. I've been offered a place at Bristol
University, but I can't afford to go unless I get a
⁴_____ (loschrapish).

Ella Good luck. I'm sure you'll get it.

Finn Thanks. What about you? What are you going to do?

Ella I'm a ⁵_____ (ylluf fiedilaqu) engineer now.
So if all goes well I'll be in ⁶_____ (lufl-mite)
work by this time next year. But in the meantime, I'm going to
take a break and enjoy travelling for a bit.

2 ★★☆ **Match the words and phrases (1–6) in Exercise 1 with the definitions (a–f).**

a an advanced college or university degree ☐

b to succeed very easily in something, especially a test ☐

c a long piece of writing on a particular subject, especially one that is done in order to receive a degree at college or university ☐

d done for the whole of a working week ☐

e having finished a training course, or having particular skills, etc. ☐

f an amount of money given by a university to pay for the studies of a person with great ability but little money ☐

Life after school

→ SB p.95

3 ★★☆ **Circle the correct verbs. Then write true answers for you.**

1 **A** Do you have to *get* / *do* military service in your country?
You _____

2 **A** Do you know anyone who *went* / *got* travelling before starting university?
You _____

3 **A** Do you know anyone who didn't *go to* / *have* university straight after school?
You _____

4 **A** Do you think it's possible to *go* / *get* a full-time job whilst you're at university?
You _____

5 **A** Do you think it's a good idea to *do* / *get* some voluntary work in the holidays?
You _____

6 **A** Do you know anyone who has *done* / *gone* an apprenticeship?
You _____

7 **A** Do you want to *go* / *take* a gap year when you finish school?
You _____

4 ★★☆ **Complete the sentences with the correct form of a verb.**

Before Orhan ¹_____ to Warwick University to study Art History he, ²_____ a gap year. After two years at Warwick, he ³_____ voluntary work at an art gallery in Mexico City during his third year. After finishing university, he returned home to Turkey and he ⁴_____ his military service. Now he wants ⁵_____ a full-time job. His brother ⁶_____ (not) to university. He ⁷_____ an apprenticeship instead. Now, he has a good job and he earns a lot of money.

5 ★★★ **Write sentences that are true for you. Use the words in brackets.**

After leaving school, …

1 (apprenticeship) _____
2 (university) _____
3 (full-time job) _____
4 (military service) _____
5 (voluntary work) _____
6 (gap year) _____

PRONUNCIATION
Lexical and non-lexical fillers
Go to page 121. 🎧

 **REFERENCE**

take a gap year

do (your) Master's degree (in)

sail through (your) exams — **Higher education** — write (your) dissertation

full-time

fully qualified

get a scholarship

 **LIFE AFTER SCHOOL**

do	take	go	get
voluntary work an apprenticeship military service	a gap year	to university	a full-time job

VOCABULARY EXTRA

1 Match the underlined words with their definitions.

1 When is our next <u>assignment</u> due?
2 I have to finish my <u>coursework</u> this week.
3 Have you got the <u>feedback</u> on your essay yet?
4 I'm not enjoying the art history <u>module</u> I chose this term.
5 Are you going to the <u>seminar</u> this afternoon?
6 I think my <u>overall mark</u> for this term will be OK.

a statements of opinion about a process or activity that can tell you if it is successful _____

b an occasion when a teacher or expert and a group of people meet to study and discuss something _____

c one of the units that together make a complete course at college or university _____

d a piece of work given to someone as part of their studies _____

e the total judgment expressed as a number or letter about the quality of all the pieces of work at school, college or university _____

f work set at regular periods as part of an educational course _____

2 Complete the dialogue with words from Exercise 1.

Eva   Hi Jakob. How's your psychology course going?

Jakob   Good, thanks. I chose a language ¹_____ this term and I'm on my way to my last ²_____ . It's about bilingual children.

Eva   Sounds interesting!

Jakob   Where are you going?

Eva   I'm going to meet my course tutor to get some ³_____ on my essay.

Jakob   I can't believe the year has almost finished. My final piece of ⁴_____ is due this week.

Eva   I know, it's gone so quickly. I have one more ⁵_____ to do and then I'll get my ⁶_____ for the whole year.

Jakob   Good luck!

3 Classify the words in Exercise 1. Can you add more words?

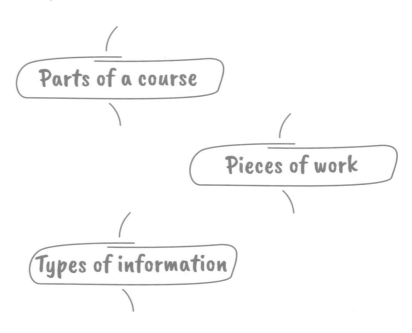

Parts of a course

Pieces of work

Types of information

TIME OUT?

A lot of people recommend taking a year off from formal education or full-time work as a way of developing practical and professional skills as well as emotional and personal awareness. Taking a break from higher education, a career and even your social life is known to be beneficial to character development. Invaluable life skills, for instance developing your emotional intelligence and gaining a greater perspective, will help you to succeed throughout the rest of your life.

If you feel tired because, for as long as you can remember, all you've done is study, take exams and move on to the next thing, then taking a year off is thought to be a good way to deal with those feelings. Maybe you feel you've lost your identity and have forgotten why you're doing whatever you're doing. Taking time out is often considered to be a great opportunity to figure out what's missing in your life and what skills you want to develop to move forward. Finding more meaning in your life means you will feel energised about whatever you decide to come back and do. So, what are the options?

VOLUNTEERING

Doing voluntary work is a good choice if you're passionate about conservation, education, or public health. It's an excellent way to find out more about yourself and the world around you as well as an issue you're keen to resolve. Combining conservation education with volunteering will allow you to learn about local communities, develop empathy and give you a more global view of your place in the world. It could help you decide if you really do want to give up a full-time job or change your future plans in order to do something different permanently.

INTERNSHIPS

These are a great way to gain new experience and learn new skills that you can't learn in your current situation. So, if you think you might want a career change from your current job or want to do something different for a short period of time while you are studying, this could be for you. Maybe you're looking to try a different industry or figure out if you're doing the right job or have chosen the right career path. If so, then an internship is a useful way to experience work without committing to it for the rest of your life! You can find internships at home or abroad so if you want to combine learning new skills in a company or organisation with going travelling, then this is a great choice.

STUDYING ABROAD

Taking time out to study is one of the best ways to learn something new and take a break. Studying abroad is a good way to change your environment, learn a new language and learn about a different culture. If you're in the workplace, then you can go back into a classroom to pursue your interests outside work or it gives you the chance to study things that you might only have dreamed of doing.

AND REMEMBER, YOU'RE NEVER TOO OLD TO LEARN AND DISCOVER NEW THINGS! SO, WHAT HAVE YOU DECIDED TO TAKE TIME OUT TO DO?

READING

1 **Read the article quickly. What is it about?**

A gap-year options for students

B the benefits of and options for a year off

C the alternatives to having a full-time job

2 **Read the article again and answer the questions.**

1 Why do some people recommend taking a year off?
_____

2 What can a year off help some people to do?
_____

3 What does volunteering teach people?
_____

4 What are the benefits of an internship?
_____

5 How can studying abroad help people in the workplace?
_____

6 What does the article say about the age limit for taking a year off?
_____

3 **CRITICAL THINKING** **Which of these quotes do you find the most meaningful? Why?**

1 'Education is the most important weapon which you can use to change the world.'

Nelson Mandela

2 'Education is not the learning of facts, but the training of the mind to think.'

Albert Einstein

3 'One child, one teacher, one book and one pen can change the world.'

Malala Yousafzai

4 **How do you think taking time out before university or during a full-time job might affect you or improve your performance? Write a short paragraph listing the advantages and disadvantages.**

DEVELOPING { *Writing*

Writing an essay

1 INPUT **Read the writing task. Which of these things do you think the essay will mention?**

Course fees ☐   Master's degrees ☐
Engineering ☐   Scholarships ☐
Gap years ☐   The school education system ☐

2 **Now read the essay and check your answers to Exercise 1.**

How can more young people be encouraged to take engineering courses at university?

1 In my opinion, there are three main reasons why students are put off studying engineering and these issues need to be addressed. Firstly, students think that you need to be good at maths to study engineering. Secondly, it is not seen as a creative or glamorous career choice. Thirdly, and perhaps most importantly, students often don't know much about engineering.

2 To address the first and second issues, I would encourage students with an interest in arts subjects to see the creative side to engineering. Show them that it isn't all about maths. Let students see the links between design and engineering – show how it is linked to other industries that young people might be interested in, such as the catering industry and hospitals. You could also show them that there are options to travel and work abroad.

3 Primary schools and secondary schools need to be given more information about what exactly engineering is and how interesting and rewarding it could be as a career. Companies could set engineering challenges for school students. Tours of work places, talks and practical projects could be given by companies. Another possibility would be to give students a financial incentive to study engineering. Lower the course fees and offer more scholarships.

4 In conclusion, I believe that firstly, engineering companies need to have more links with schools to show children exactly what engineering entails and to show them it can be just as exciting and creative a career as journalism or architecture. Secondly, the government needs to create financial incentives to study engineering as it is important for this country's future.

Read the quote and then write an essay to answer the question.
'British industry needs 40,000 more scientists, engineers and technicians each year, forcing many companies to seek out highly-trained people from overseas to fill the vacancies in the workforce.'

3 ANALYSE **In which paragraph does the writer ...**

1 suggest different ways to encourage more students to study engineering? ☐
2 state that engineering companies need to show young people that engineering is an exciting career? ☐
3 give their opinion about why students don't study engineering? ☐
4 explain how schools and companies could help each other? ☐

4 PLAN **Choose one of the careers below or use your own idea. Think about how you would encourage school students to choose this career. Read the tip box and make notes.**

> archaeology | architecture | art history
> business and management | film and theatre
> law | marine biology | medicine | teaching
> translation | transportation planning

You may use some of the ideas expressed in the sample essay, but you should use your own ideas as far as possible. Think about how to motivate students and what incentives you could give.

 WRITING TIP: AN ESSAY

Before writing, make a list of all the possible ways to encourage students. For example, architecture:

- Take students on visits to see buildings of interest in your town.
- Look at your school or college. Is it well designed? Which features and facilities work well?
- What could be improved?
- Organise a design competition: Design a building.
- Study materials used in building.

5 PRODUCE **Write your essay (220–280 words). Use your notes from Exercise 4 and the information in the tip box. Make your own checklist.**

✓ CHECKLIST

☐ _____

☐ _____

🎧 LISTENING

1 🔊 **10.02** **Listen to the conversation between three friends and note down four reasons given for banning mobile phones.**

1 _____
   _____
2 _____
   _____
3 _____
   _____
4 _____
   _____

2 🔊 **10.02** **Listen to the dialogue again. Mark the sentences T (true), F (false) or DS (doesn't say).**

1 Max is not happy to hear that mobile phones will be banned from school. ☐

2 Emma says it's hard for students to concentrate in class when they are allowed to use their mobile phones. ☐

3 Emma says students' grades would improve if they didn't use mobile phones in school. ☐

4 Most mobile phones are stolen from students aged between 13 and 16. ☐

5 One in fifteen children aged eight to 16 will have their mobile phone stolen. ☐

6 There is a danger that a child texting while crossing the road may be involved in an accident. ☐

7 Max thinks banning mobile phones will just cause more problems. ☐

8 The mobile phone ban will be put into practice next year. ☐

DIALOGUE

1 **Complete the dialogues with the phrases in the list.**

> I'm glad to hear it
> I think it's about time
> That's outrageous
> That's the best news I've heard in ages
> They've got to be joking
> What will they think of next

1

Mel Have you heard the fast food restaurant opposite school is being closed down? Apparently, the school has complained about it being there. They say it encourages students to make bad food choices.

Sara ¹_____? Take away the vending machine, too? I think we should be able to choose what we want to eat.

Mel Personally, ²_____ . The food there is horrible – plastic burgers in plastic buns and horrible greasy chips. I don't think there's any real meat in the burgers.

Sara How would you know? You're a vegetarian.

2

Mateo ³_____ they did something about the school Chemistry lab. All the equipment in there is falling to pieces.

Sarina Haven't you heard? Mr Morris took it up with the school board last week and some money is being allocated to buying new equipment.

Mateo ⁴_____ . But how did you find out about it?

Sarina I've been complaining to my mum about it for months. She was at the meeting last week and she told me.

Mateo Why didn't you tell me earlier then?

3

Amy I'm afraid I've got some bad news for you, Leo.

Leo What now?

Amy The school isn't letting anyone take A-Level Art as of next year.

Leo ⁵_____ , surely! The only reason I want to stay on at school is to take Art.

Amy I knew you'd be upset.

Leo ⁶_____ . They'll be cancelling Music lessons and P.E. soon, I expect.

Amy They can't do that.

Leo If they can cancel Art lessons for sixth formers, they can cancel Music. You wait, that will be next on the list.

2 **Write a new dialogue. Complain to a friend about something that has happened or will happen at school that you disagree with. Include phrases from Exercise 1.**

C1 Advanced

LISTENING
Part 4: Multiple matching

⟶ SB p.100

EXAM GUIDE:

In Listening Part 4, you will hear five speakers talk about a common topic. For this task, you will need to listen out for the speaker's opinion, attitude or feeling about something. You will need to answer two sets of questions and you will only hear each extract twice.

- Read both sets of questions first.
- Remember, there are three extra options that you won't use in each task.
- Listen for similar themes: Is it about the past or the future? This will help you in choosing the answers.
- While you listen, you must complete both tasks.

---

1 🔊 10.03 You will hear five short extracts in which university students are talking about their studies.

Task One
For questions 1–5, choose from the list (A–H) each speaker's reason for choosing their particular course of study.

A the reputation of the academic staff

B recommendations from existing students

C the study facilities available to students

D the convenience of the location

E what former students have gone on to do

F the experience of a reliable person

G the appearance of the campus

H the chance to get practical experience

1 Speaker 1 ☐

2 Speaker 2 ☐

3 Speaker 3 ☐

4 Speaker 4 ☐

5 Speaker 5 ☐

Task Two
For questions 6–10, choose from the list (A–H) what has surprised each speaker most about their course so far.

A how much background reading is required

B the attitude of the other students

C the range of topic areas covered

D the chance to get involved in important research

E the effectiveness of the teaching methods

F how easy it is to develop personal interests

G the way work is assessed

H the type of technology available

6 Speaker 1 ☐

7 Speaker 2 ☐

8 Speaker 3 ☐

9 Speaker 4 ☐

10 Speaker 5 ☐

CONSOLIDATION

🎧 LISTENING

1 🔊 **10.04** **Listen to a man complaining about something. What does he think is unfair?**

_____

2 🔊 **10.04** **Listen again and answer the questions.**

1 Why were the queues for some rides really long?

_____

2 While he was in the queue, what did the man see that he described as 'odd'?

_____

3 How does the queue jumper work?

_____

4 Why does the man think the queue jumper system is unfair?

_____

5 What do some airports offer that annoys the man?

_____

6 What is the man's overall opinion about money?

_____

Ⓖ GRAMMAR

3 **Put the words in order to make sentences.**

1 insisted / washing / me / on / doing / Mum / the / up / .

_____

2 of / silly / At / the / day / only / it's / a / the / game / end / .

_____

3 the / for / TV / Dad / me / blamed / breaking / .

_____

4 I / apologise / will / circumstances / to / Under / Maria / no / .

_____

5 been / the / believed / to / He / involved / in / robbery / is / have / .

_____

6 It's / solved / the / never / might / thought / that / mystery / be / .

_____

7 I / in / the / No / shower / had / than / the / sooner / phone / rang / got / .

_____

🔤 VOCABULARY

4 **Match the sentence halves.**

1 My mother had to go to court to give ☐

2 He's smart and we expect he'll sail ☐

3 Because of the seriousness of the crime, he was ☐

4 I'm considering taking ☐

5 He felt so guilty he made ☐

6 My parents couldn't afford that school, but I got ☐

7 She spends every Saturday doing ☐

8 My brother's writing his ☐

a sentenced to life imprisonment.

b a confession to the police.

c dissertation on Eastern European politics.

d evidence in a trial.

e voluntary work helping with the elderly.

f a gap year before I go to university.

g a scholarship and studied there for free.

h through his end of year exams.

5 **Complete the sentences with the words in the list.**

> equal | evident | general | obese
> political | social | unfair | violent

1 Which _____ party do you agree with most?

2 Society is _____ when there is a big difference between rich people and everyone else.

3 How can we reduce _____ crime in our city?

4 There are a lot of causes of _____ problems – poverty is one of them.

5 In _____ , people who live in warmer countries are happier and healthier.

6 Being _____ is often a sign of other issues.

7 In my opinion, it is _____ that there is a connection between the weather and climate change.

8 _____ rights for men and women is still a problem in a lot of situations.

DIALOGUE

6 **Complete the dialogue with the phrases in the list. There are two you do not need.**

> action | be joking | do that | or less |
> or take | outrageous | region | something

Rob It's going to cost you £30,000 more ¹_____ if you want to go to university.

Alicia £30,000? That's ²_____ .

Rob And that's only for tuition. With accommodation and food you're looking at ³_____ like £50,000.

Alicia That's absurd.

Rob And now universities are increasing their fees even more.

Alicia That's not fair. They can't ⁴_____ .

Rob No, they can't, which is why we're organising a protest next week.

Alicia Finally, someone's taking ⁵_____ .

Rob Yes, we're expecting something in the ⁶_____ of 100,000 students to join.

Alicia Well, make that 100,001 because I'm definitely going.

 ## READING

7 **Read the article and complete the table.**

	rule	reason
food		
language		
recreation		
clothing		

Every school needs a solid set of rules which help guide their students and let them know what will and won't be tolerated. Most school rules are based on a set of sound and sensible principles. However, occasionally there are cases when schools have been known to take things one step too far. Here are some of the more interesting cases to have made it into the papers.

A school in Essex has banned its canteen servers from serving a type of biscuit known as flapjack in the shape of a triangle. The decision was reached after a student was hit in the face by a piece of triangular flapjack that had been thrown by another pupil. From now on, flapjack must be cut into square or rectangular portions.

Another school in Croydon, London has banned its students from using slang. On the list of forbidden items are words such as 'ain't' (is not), 'innit' (isn't it), 'coz' (because) and 'you/we woz'. The school took the decision in an attempt to make their students more employable. The school believes that students who use such informal language will find it more difficult to get jobs when they leave.

Morning break has long been a time when students can release all the energy they've stored up while sitting in lessons by playing football or some other activity involving running around the playground for half an hour. Not any more for students at a school in Connecticut, US, which has put a ban on such activities as the authorities fear they could provoke physical or emotional damage. Instead students are encouraged to jump ropes or gently throw frisbees. Supervised games of 'kickball' are occasionally allowed but only if the score is not kept.

Clothing is often an area of controversy and there are many stories of students who have been sent home because their clothes contravene what's acceptable within the school rules. But one of the more unusual items to have been banned are UGG-type boots. Winters in Pennsylvania can be extremely cold and these fur-lined boots could be seen as the ideal footwear for keeping students' feet warm and dry. Not so, according to one school in the area, which has forbidden students from wearing them to school. The reason? Apparently, they offer the perfect place for smuggling mobile phones into the school!

 ## WRITING

8 **Invent a crazy school rule. Write an announcement explaining the rule and the reasons for it.**

GRAMMAR
More on the passive
→ SB p.104

1 ★☆☆ **Circle the correct verbs. Sometimes both options are possible.**

1 We *were / got* soaked walking home in the rain.
2 When she tried to leave, she discovered the door *was / got* locked.
3 Tom told his mother he didn't know how the TV *was / got* broken.
4 Sally ran into the road without looking and *was / got* hit by a car.
5 She *was / got* loved by everyone who knew her.
6 My case *was / got* put on the wrong plane and went to China!

2 ★★☆ **Replace the verb *be* with *get* where possible.**

1 Some strange lights were seen in the sky and there was a lot of talk of UFOs.
2 Gilly was stopped for speeding by a police patrol.
3 You might be mugged if you wear a gold watch on that beach.
4 James was heard talking to his girlfriend on the office phone.
5 After his interview on TV, Steve was phoned by a lot of people he didn't know.
6 When my mother tidied my bedroom, some of my favourite things were thrown away.

3 ★★★ **Rewrite these sentences, starting with the words given. Use *get* wherever possible.**

1 Someone stole my suitcase while I was asleep.
   My suitcase _____ .
2 Helen's mother told her off for being late home.
   Helen _____ .
3 Somebody saw the man leaving the bank with a bag.
   The man _____ .
4 Some kids throwing stones hurt my cat.
   My cat _____ .
5 My grandmother loved the new baby.
   The new baby _____ .
6 People talk about film stars a lot.
   Film stars _____ .

Causative *have* (review)
→ SB p.105

4 ★★☆ **Complete the gaps with the correct form of *have* and the verbs given.**

0 My hair's too long. I must _____*have*_____ it _____*cut*_____ . (cut)
1 My car needs a paint job. I will _____ it _____ . (repaint)
2 The carpet was very dirty. We _____ it _____ . (clean)
3 Their garden wall was damaged in the accident. They _____ it _____ . (rebuild)
4 The old garage was falling down, so we had to _____ it _____ . (demolish)
5 Lucy broke her tooth and it was causing her a lot of pain, so she _____ it _____ by the dentist. (take out)

5 ★★☆ **Complete the dialogue with the correct form of *have* and the words in the list.**

changed | installed | painted
put in | repaired | replaced

Jamal Hi, Harry! I heard your parents' new house was broken into. How awful! Was anything stolen?

Harry No, but they had ¹_____ a new back door _____ before we could move in. And, of course, they needed to ²_____ the locks _____ .

Jamal When did you all eventually move in?

Harry Last month. They ³_____ the roof _____ first – there were a lot of broken tiles.

Jamal What about the windows?

Harry They ⁴_____ two of them _____ , but the others were OK apparently. They just needed painting.

Jamal ⁵_____ they _____ them _____ ?

Harry No, my parents did the painting themselves.

Jamal What about inside?

Harry That's almost done now. My mum and dad ⁶_____ just _____ a new kitchen _____ .

Jamal Wow! That's a lot of work for your parents.

Harry I know. I just had to sort my bedroom out!

Modal passives (review)   → SB p.107

6 ★☆☆ **Circle the correct answers.**

1 Her face *will never be / will never have been* forgotten.

2 This pie *must be / must have been heated* before it is eaten.

3 The building *might be / might have been* demolished because it wasn't safe.

4 A new theatre *may be / may have been* built soon.

5 Don't throw those old clothes away – they *can be / can have been* reused.

6 The child *shouldn't be / shouldn't have been* left alone – the accident *might be / might have been* avoided.

7 The students *must be / must have been* told the rules before the test begins.

8 By the end of this year she *will be / will have been* seen in three new films.

7 ★★☆ **Put the words in italics in the correct order .**

0 I dropped my phone in the bath and the shop says *repaired / be / it / can't*
   <u>it can't be repaired.</u>

1 The writing on the notice was so bad *have / a child / by / could / it / written / been*
   _____ .

2 This medicine is for adults and *to / children / given / should / be / not*
   _____ .

3 I didn't recognise her in the play – *dyed / hair / have / her / been / must*
   _____ .

4 You've done that wrong! *red / first / should / been / pressed / button / The / have*
   _____ .

5 Why are you taking your tablet with you? *only / can / used / in / with / places / wi-fi / be / It*
   _____ .

6 Don't phone the bank yet. *be / questions / website / might / on / Your / the / answered*
   _____ .

7 The vegetables smell awful; *they / have / fridge / should / kept / in / the / been*
   _____ .

8 If I'd told my parents the truth *stopped / have / allowance / a / would / month / my / for / been*
   _____ .

8 ★★☆ **Complete the sentences. Use the modal passive form of the verbs.**

1 The TV is working, so it _____ away. (must not / throw)

2 These plastic bottles _____ into all sorts of different things. (can / make)

3 Those old-fashioned dresses _____ by a film star in the 1950s. (might / wear)

4 That picture _____ by my grandfather – he was an artist. (could / paint)

5 This film _____ by millions of people over the coming months. (will / see)

6 The biscuits _____ in an air-tight box. (should / store)

7 This purse _____ here by that old lady. She was sitting on this seat. (may / leave)

8 That old doll _____ by many different children over the years. (must / love)

GET IT *RIGHT!*

Causative *have*

Learners often make mistakes with word order when using causative *have*. Another typical learner error is the failure to use causative *have*, opting for the active form.

✓ I had my hair cut.

✗ I had cut my hair.

✗ I cut my hair.

Rewrite the sentences correctly.

1 Jonah had fixed his bike at the bike shop last week.
   _____

2 My mum has dyed her hair once a month.
   _____

3 George has had stolen his phone at school. He's furious!
   _____

4 Peter is going check his eyes tomorrow at the hospital.
   _____

5 Ben wants to take his laptop into the shop to repair it.
   _____

6 We should have had cut down the tree before it blew over in the wind.
   _____

VOCABULARY
(not) getting angry
⟶ SB p.104

1 ★☆☆ **Read the sentences. Did the person get angry or not? Mark the sentences A (angry) or NA (not angry).**

1 I got so worked up that I had to tell her what I thought.

2 I told him what was on my mind – I just had to let off steam.

3 I think I kind of bit his head off yesterday. I hope he's not too upset with me.

4 I'm really proud of the way I kept my cool in that meeting today.

5 I've never seen Jack lose his temper like that before.

6 They just shouted at me for about ten minutes.

7 Fortunately, she stayed calm and everything was OK a few minutes later.

8 I didn't like what she was saying at all, but I bit my tongue and left.

9 It wasn't easy to keep the peace between us, but I think I managed to do it.

10 I was late for class again and Mr Bell really had a go at me.

2 ★★☆ **Complete the sentences with words from the list.**

cool | go | head | peace | shout | stay
steam | temper | tongue | up

1 Please don't _____ at me like that!

2 I really don't like it when you lose your _____ like that.

3 Just try not to get so worked _____ about unimportant things.

4 The essential thing at times like this is to keep your _____ , OK?

5 Sometimes it's helpful to let off _____ .

6 The teacher got really mad and had a _____ at the whole class.

7 Don't say anything! I know it's awful but just bite your _____ , OK?

8 Let's do our best to keep the _____ between them.

9 He shouted at her and well, he really bit her _____ off.

10 _____ calm and answer the questions as best you can.

PRONUNCIATION
Intonation: mean what you say Go to page 121. 🎧

---

3 ★★★ **Complete the sentences so they are true for you.**

1 _____ is very good at keeping the peace.

2 _____ shouted at me when I _____ .

3 It's sometimes hard for me to keep my cool when _____ .

4 Once I had a go at someone who _____ .

5 I always have to bite my tongue when _____ .

-isms
⟶ SB p.107

4 ★☆☆ **Match the words with the definitions to complete the puzzle.**

ageism | capitalism | optimism
pessimism | socialism

1 _____ the set of beliefs that states that all people are equal and should share equally in a country's money or political systems

2 _____ the feeling that good things are going to happen

3 _____ unfair treatment of people because of their age

4 _____ economic, political and social system in which property, business and industry are privately owned and directed towards making the most profit

5 _____ the feeling that bad things are going to happen

5 ★★☆ **Choose the correct words.**

1 *I believe in* socialism / capitalism *because I think it's important that we live in a society where everyone is equal.*

2 *There is a mood of* capitalism / pessimism *across the whole country as the lockdown continues.*

3 *I think that* ageism / optimism *affects young and old more than they realise.*

4 Capitalism / Pessimism *is a political ideology that makes rich people richer and poor people poorer.*

5 *There was a note of* ageism / optimism *in her voice as she spoke to the people about the development of a vaccine.*

REFERENCE

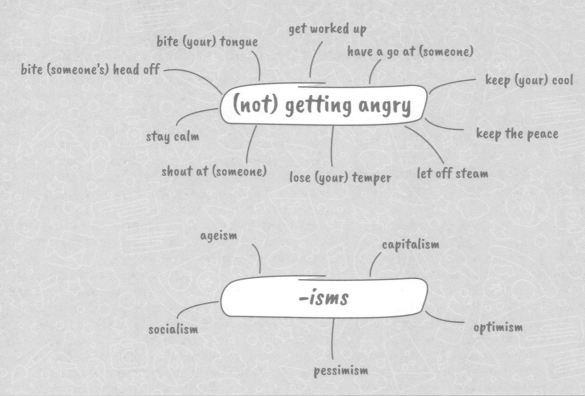

VOCABULARY EXTRA

1 Match the expressions in bold in the sentences (1–6) with the definitions (a–f).

1 I **have a sneaking suspicion** you might be correct. ☐
2 The police **have reason to believe** you were involved in an accident. ☐
3 I **share your opinion** on lowering the voting age to 16. ☐
4 We had **a difference of opinion** with Elise about the exam questions. ☐
5 We**'re poles apart** in our views on politics. ☐
6 I **firmly believe** that young people can make a difference through their actions. ☐

a to have the same opinion as other people
b to have completely opposite views or opinions
c to have a strong opinion or belief that is unlikely to change
d to have a feeling about someone or something which you are not sure about
e to disagree with someone
f to feel justified in thinking or believing

2 Put the words in order to make sentences.

1 opinion / don't / literature / parents / my / on / My / share

_____

2 owner / reason / We / this / believe / you / have / are / vehicle / of / to/ the

_____

3 suspicion / win / you / sneaking / I / a / have / will

_____

4 revision / apart / our / We're / attitude / poles / in / to

_____

5 opinion / career choice / I / a / of / my / with / family / about / had / my / difference

_____

6 us / that / listen / firmly / the / believe / government / to / will / We

_____

3 Complete the sentences so they are true for you.

1 I have a difference of opinion with … about …
2 I have a sneaking suspicion that …
3 I'm poles apart in my views on … with …

YOUR VIEWS COUNT
FAIRNESS AND EQUALITY?

I'm sure you've heard of socialism, capitalism and ageism, but have you ever heard of youngism? If you haven't, then, like me, you've probably experienced it but maybe without realising. It's a prejudice against teenagers and young people and if you look around, you might be surprised to find that it's happening all around you.

Last week for example, I was about to go into a shop when I saw a notice on the door: 'Only two students allowed in at any time.' I got really worked up about it and decided not to go into the shop. My friend went in, but she managed to bite her tongue and keep her cool. Can you imagine what would happen if the notice had said 'Only two pensioners allowed' instead? The signs would have been removed very quickly. Retailers somehow feel they can get away with it because it's young people. It's just not right. Some shop owners often claim that the notices are there because they are trying to reduce shoplifting and protect their business and profits. What they mean is they think teenagers shoplift more than adults. This is completely wrong. According to statistics, due to poverty and other social issues, adults are more likely to shoplift. So, is the answer banning people over the age of 18 from shops? I don't think so.

In schools, young people are often not treated with respect. Our views are not taken seriously by teachers or governments and we are not allowed to choose our own curriculum. We are often not offered much practical advice or life skills lessons, so some of us are unprepared for life as an adult. We can't become more active citizens if we haven't been given the chance to do so from a young age.

We are also treated differently in other parts of society. For example, we're not given the same political rights as adults. In my opinion, voting for 16- and 17-year-olds should be obligatory. We are the future, but if we aren't allowed to change the present, how can we make a difference in the future? The vast majority of young people care deeply about social and political issues and we want to fight for change – not just for ourselves, but for young people everywhere. Some people have said that our optimism is contagious, and we should be listened to, but those words seem to have fallen on deaf ears.

Young people are often paid less than adults for doing the same jobs, so they are discriminated against in the workplace, too. I work part-time in a local department store and I often have to listen to older colleagues telling me that young people don't know what hard work is. Younger employees are often described as arrogant, lazy or even stupid by older colleagues. Imagine if I had said that about an older person I was working with. I'd have lost my job. Older people are often not prepared to give us a chance to prove ourselves and to show that we not only have stamina, but we are also very committed.

So why are young people still subjected to this form of prejudice in the 21st century? Maybe it's time we stood up for ourselves and stopped biting our tongues every time we're treated unfairly. Next time you experience youngism, stay calm and make sure the person treating you unfairly is made aware of their actions and the consequences.

 What do you think? Post your comments now.

READING

1 **Read the text quickly. What is it about?**

A discrimination against old people ☐

B discrimination against young people ☐

C the differences between young and old people ☐

2 **Read the text again. Mark the sentences T (true) or F (false). Correct the false sentences.**

1 Youngism is a prejudice against older people. ☐

2 The writer found a notice in a shop very offensive. ☐

3 Teenagers are less likely to shoplift than adults. ☐

4 The writer thinks that it's acceptable for older people to be rude about younger people. ☐

5 The writer thinks young people should be allowed to vote. ☐

6 According to the writer, young people should learn to bite their tongues when they experience youngism. ☐

3 CRITICAL THINKING **Answer the questions.**

1 What did you know about youngism before you read the text?

2 Has your opinion changed now? Why? / Why not?

3 What is the effect of youngism on young people, in your opinion?

4 **Think of a time you or someone you know experienced youngism. Write a short paragraph describing the situation.**

_____

_____

_____

_____

_____

_____

DEVELOPING Writing

Writing a blog post

1 **INPUT** **Read Josie's blog post and answer the questions.**

1 What three areas did people suggest were better now than in the 1980s and 1990s?
2 What area of life is more stressful now than in the past?
3 What subject might the writer deal with next?

Josie's blog – just how hard is life these days?

About | **New posts** **Archives**

Have you ever wondered what life is like now compared to, say, the 1980s or the 1990s? I went and talked to some people I know who were adults during those decades and I asked them. The answer I got was that overall, life's a lot better now! Which didn't really surprise me. I mean, these days we've got mobile phones and the internet and so on – but actually, those weren't the things they talked about.

So what did they talk about? For a start, people felt that life is better these days because we don't have to work so physically hard since there are more efficient household appliances to do the housework and other boring chores. Then there's the matter of how, these days, it's possible to work at home – and OK, it's mainly computers and stuff that have made this possible, but even so, it means that a lot of

people don't have to spend so much of their lives just going to and from work every day.

Not only that, but there's a lot more equality now. The situation isn't perfect, of course, but I think it's easier for all people, whatever their social background, gender, colour and so on, to have equal access to a variety of career opportunities.

That said, it's not all a matter of improvements. Quite a few people told me that they feel more stressed these days because they rely a lot on technology and they worry about security on the internet. Plus, we do spend a lot of our time with tablets and smartphones, don't we? One person said, 'Wouldn't it be great to go off grid for a few days?' Hmm, not so sure about that one! But maybe I'll give it a try – and then write about it on my next blog post!

---

2 **ANALYSE** **Read the blog again. Find these things.**

1 a phrase Josie uses to introduce the first thing people talked about _____
2 three words or phrases Josie uses to introduce additional points _____
3 a phrase Josie uses to introduce a contrasting point _____

3 **In blogs, people often write informally. Find at least three more examples of informal language in the blog.**

OK, I mean, _____ ,
_____ , _____

4 **PLAN** **Imagine you are Josie and you decided to not go online for five days. What do you think would be the good and the bad points about this? Make notes.**

5 **PRODUCE** **Write a blog post (250–300 words). Start your blog with the sentences below. Use language from Exercises 2 and 3 and your notes from Exercise 4. Make your own checklist.**

OK, I did it! Five days off the grid! Now I'm back and I want to tell you what it was like …

✔ CHECKLIST

- [ ] _____
- [ ] _____
- [ ] _____
- [ ] _____
- [ ] _____

🎧 LISTENING

1 🔊 **11.02** **Listen to a radio interview about 'modern teenagers'. Number the things below in the order that the woman mentions them.**

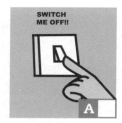

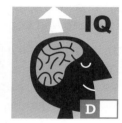

2 🔊 **11.02** **Listen again. Answer the questions.**

1 Why is the ability to analyse things increasing amongst teenagers?

2 How has the rate of teenage violence changed over the last decade?

3 How does that rate compare to the rate for older people?

4 Why is an increase in environmental awareness 'to be expected'?

5 What kind of things do teenagers volunteer for?

6 In what way do teenagers now differ from previous generations with regard to their parents?

DIALOGUE

1 **Put the dialogues in order. Then complete the dialogues with one word in each gap.**

1

☐ Marco So, don't – just smile and think about something else. Or better, start talking about something else.

☐ Marco I get that a lot from my family too. Just don't let it ¹_____ to you.

☑ Marco What on earth's the matter with you? You look really fed up!

☐ Sonia Yes, you're right. But it's not always that easy to smile. I just need to chill ²_____ a bit, I reckon.

☐ Sonia I've just been listening to my uncle and aunt going on about how terrible teenagers are these days.

☐ Sonia Well I try not to, but sometimes it makes me so mad. And they're nice people – I like them a lot, so I don't want to argue with them.

2

☐ Stevie I suppose you're right. After all, there are worse things in life than spam, aren't there?

☐ Stevie I suppose not. But sometimes I get so angry that I write back with something rude.

☐ Stevie Me too. I hate those emails, trying to sell me something or trying to trick me. It drives me crazy.

☐ Esther I know. But I try not to get angry – there's no point in getting worked ³_____ , is there?

☑ Esther I seem to be getting more and more spam in my inbox these days.

☐ Esther Oh that's the worst thing you can do! Then they know that your email address really exists. You need to calm ⁴_____ and just hit the delete button.

3

☐ Jason Well, that's easier said than done – we're in the same class, so how can I avoid her?

☐ Jason It's not what she's done, it's what she's said. Another nasty comment about my sister. She's clearly trying her best to annoy me – and it's working.

☑ Jason I'm never going to talk to Judy again! I've had enough!

☐ Harry Sit as far away as possible and look in other directions – that's what I'd do, anyway.

☐ Harry Hey, take it ⁵_____ , Jason. What's she done?

☐ Harry Look, don't let her get under your ⁶_____ , OK?

2 **Write a short dialogue (6–8 lines). Use one of the lines below.**

1 I don't see why you're losing your temper with me!

2 And then she really bit his head off.

3 I tried not to lose my cool, but it didn't work.

4 Don't let them get under your skin, OK?

C1 Advanced

READING AND USE OF ENGLISH
Part 3: Word formation

EXAM GUIDE:

In Part 3 of the Reading and Use of English exam, you are given a text with eight gaps. At the end of some lines, there is a word in capital letters. You have to form a word based on the word in capital letters to fit in the gap. For example, you may need to change a noun (*happiness*) into an adjective (*happy*) or an adverb (*happily*).

- Occasionally, you will have to produce a negative word from a positive one. For example, you may need to add a prefix to a word (*legal*) to make it negative (*illegal*).

- Be careful – sometimes a question will be written in a way where you perhaps will think you need an adjective but in fact you need an adverb. For example, in the question 'It was a … beautiful place' (STUNNING), this would need to be an adverb, 'It was a <u>stunningly</u> beautiful place.'

1   For questions 1–8, read the text below. Use the word given in capitals at the end of some of the lines to form a word that fits in the gap in the same line. There is an example at the beginning (0).

Any attempt to compare life in the twenty-first century with that of
a hundred years ago is doomed to **(0)** *failure* . This is principally   **FAIL**
because, especially in the early part of this century, the rate of
(1) _____ change has been so rapid. The things that we   **TECHNOLOGY**
use now on a daily basis are tools that, for our grandparents, would have
been completely **(2)** _____ . Phone technology, in   **IMAGINE**
particular, has developed at an **(3)** _____ rapid rate.   **ASTONISH**
Almost every day we learn about a new **(4)** _____ which   **INNOVATE**
offers yet further so-called **(5)** _____ in the way we   **IMPROVE**
communicate with each other. Yet one might argue that our
(6) _____ for such advances, given the levels of poverty   **ENTHUSE**
and hunger in the world, is **(7)** _____ . Will we be   **JUSTIFY**
remembered as the generation whose love of the latest gadgets destroyed
our compassion and **(8)** _____ for one another?   **CONSIDER**

12 CELEBRATING HEROES

Grammar video ▶31

@ GRAMMAR
Future perfect; future continuous (review)
→ SB p.112

1 ★★☆ **Write sentences. Use the future perfect or future continuous forms of the verbs.**

This time next year …

1 my brother / still / travel / around / Mexico

_____

2 I / still / study / History / at / university

_____

3 my sister Elena / finish / her / degree

_____

4 Elena / still / look / for / a / job

_____

5 my family / move / house

_____

6 we / live / in / our / new / house

_____

2 ★★☆ **Complete the sentences with the future perfect form of the verbs**

THE HOLIDAY OF A LIFETIME

By the time you leave Ecuador and the Galápagos Islands …

1 you _____ (hike) up two volcanoes.

2 you _____ (travel) up the Amazon to remote villages by canoe.

3 you _____ (be) whale watching.

4 you _____ (see) the glacier that covers the peak of Cotopaxi.

5 you _____ (explore) the famous indigenous market of Otavalo.

6 you _____ (experience) standing with your feet in two hemispheres on the equator line at Mitad Del Mundo.

7 you _____ (have) the holiday of a lifetime.

3 ★★☆ **What will you be doing next year? Answer the questions. Write long answers.**

1 **A** Where will you be living?
   You _____

2 **A** What will you be studying?
   You _____

3 **A** Will you have left school?
   You _____

4 **A** What sports will you be playing?
   You _____

5 **A** Will you have taken any important exams?
   You _____

6 **A** Will you be learning to play any musical instruments?
   You _____

4 ★★☆ **Use the future perfect or future continuous forms of the verbs in the list to complete Daniel's six-point plan for the future.**

| complete | make | open |
| queue | start | think |

I have always loved making cakes. Here is my six-point plan for the future.

0 In five years' time, I *will have opened a bakery* .

1 People _____ up to buy my cakes.

2 I _____ a good profit in the first year.

3 In the second year, I _____ of opening a second shop.

4 By the end of the third year, I _____ a bread-making course.

5 By the end of the following year, I _____ to sell bread as well as cakes.

5 ★★★ **Write a six-point plan like Daniel's.**

In ten years' time …

1 _____

2 _____

3 _____

4 _____

5 _____

6 _____

Future in the past

 SB p.115

6 ★★☆ **Complete the sentences with *was/wasn't/ were going to* or *would/wouldn't*.**

I had so many nice plans for this weekend.
I ¹_____ (play) basketball on Saturday morning. Then my friends and I ²_____ (have) lunch together at our favourite Italian restaurant. After that, I ³_____ (do) some shopping in town. My friend Tina said she ⁴_____ (probably come) with me. However, I didn't think she ⁵_____ (have) time, as I know she's got lots of homework to do this weekend. In the evening, I ⁶_____ (see) a Spanish film at the new cinema with my brother. My parents ⁷_____ (come) with us, but I knew they ⁸_____ (not want) to see the same film. I don't actually think they ⁹_____ (have) the patience to read the subtitles! Maybe after the film, we ¹⁰_____ (go) and get something to eat together as a family.
Now here I am in hospital with a broken leg, so I won't be doing any of those things!

7 ★★☆ **Rewrite the sentences using *was/were going to* or *would*.**

0 Stef wanted to go to the comedy show last night. He couldn't go because it was cancelled.
Stef was going to go to the comedy show last night but it was cancelled.

1 Kyllian intended to message you this afternoon, but then his phone ran out of battery.
_____

2 I didn't expect my brother to leave home so soon after he finished school.
I didn't think _____ .

3 We hadn't planned to volunteer to do the beach clean-up, but now we are glad we did.
_____

4 They planned to visit some friends in Italy this summer, but then the friends came to visit them instead.
_____

5 My parents expected me to be late home, but not this late.
My parents thought _____
probably _____ .

6 I didn't expect to pass the History exam, so I was surprised when I got such a good mark.
I didn't think _____ .

7 Ana had booked to do a cooking course next week. Now she can't go because she's broken her arm.
_____

8 ★★★ **Have you ever made plans and then had to break them? Write some of your plans here. Use *was/were going to*.**

I was going to go to university, but then I got offered an apprenticeship at an advertising firm.
My brother and I were going to have a piano lesson last night, but we missed the bus.

1 _____
2 _____
3 _____
4 _____
5 _____

GET IT RIGHT!

Future continuous and future perfect

Learners often use the future simple when the future perfect or future continuous is required.

✓ This time next year I will be doing a degree in English at Cambridge University.

✗ This time next year I ~~will do~~ a degree in English at Cambridge University.

✓ This time next year I will have finished my school exams and be at university.

✗ This time next year I ~~will finish~~ my school exams and be at university.

Rewrite the sentences about the future in a more appropriate form – future continuous or future perfect.

1 I won't be at the lecture tomorrow. Perhaps the day after tomorrow I can borrow your notes on what you will do tomorrow.
_____

2 All of next week we will campaign for the fight against child poverty.
_____

3 By next Saturday the final candidates will be shortlisted.
_____

4 The moment Eve appears on stage tomorrow, her lifelong ambition will be fulfilled.
_____

5 Next Tuesday the whole country will vote in the general election.
_____

6 I will lie on the beach and relax this time next month.
_____

 **VOCABULARY**
Awards

→ SB p.112

1 ★★☆ **Complete the dialogues with the correct form of the verbs in the list.**

> be in the running for | campaign for
> elect | nominate | put forward for
> shortlist | vote for

1 **A** I _____ your name _____ the local environmental hero award.
  B Really? But I don't think I stand a chance. There are so many other candidates.

2 **A** Leyla _____ the Green Party last year.
  B Yes, I heard she delivered leaflets and she knocked on people's doors and talked to them.

3 **A** Who did you _____ in the election?
  B Tom Jackson but he _____ . He didn't win many votes, unfortunately.

4 **A** Did you know Tony Smithson _____ the director's post?
  B Yes, I did. He told me he _____ . Apparently, they've chosen five candidates to interview out of the 15 applicants.

5 **A** Who did you _____ for the Henry Moore Sculpture Award?
  B You, actually. I think you've done some great work this term.

Success and failure

→ SB p.113

2 ★★☆ **Circle the correct phrases.**

1 **A** Has Alex done that motorcycle stunt yet?
  B No, he hasn't. It's a very difficult stunt to *overcome his adversity / pull off*.

2 **A** Did you manage to climb Ben Nevis last weekend?
  B Yes, I *fulfilled my ambition of / was recognised as* climbing the highest mountain in the UK.

3 **A** Did the stuntman jump over ten buses on his motorcycle?
  B No, he *failed spectacularly / pulled it off* but luckily he wasn't hurt.

4 **A** Is Rafa still going to Mexico this winter?
  B No, *he didn't give up on his dream / his plans fell through*. He couldn't raise enough money for the trip.

5 **A** Does Lisa still want to swim across the English Channel?
  B Yes, she does. She *has fulfilled her ambition / hasn't given up on her dream* yet.

6 **A** Antonio has done really well, hasn't he?
  B Yes, he *is recognised as / plans fell through* one of the most talented young divers in the UK.

3 ★★★ **Write a sentence about each of the following.**

1 an ambition you have fulfilled
_____

2 a dream you would like to pursue
_____

3 something you have failed spectacularly at
_____

WordWise: Expressions with *in*

→ SB p.115

4 ★★☆ **Complete the dialogues with the words in the list.**

> eye | mind | particular | spite | time

1 **A** Is it this colour in _____ that you want or shall I show you the shirt in another colour?
  B No, I just want the shirt in this colour.

2 **A** It must be very difficult to be a famous actor. I'd hate to be in the public _____ all the time.
  B Oh, really? I think I'd quite enjoy it.

3 **A** Is this the kind of day out you had in _____ ?
  B Yes, it is. I've loved every minute of it. Thanks so much for organising it.

4 **A** Did you have a good holiday?
  B Yes, thanks. In _____ of the wet weather we had a great time.

5 **A** Do you think you can mend my bike for me? I've got to be home by 5 pm.
  B No worries. We'll have it ready for you in no _____ .

PRONUNCIATION
Shifting word stress Go to page 121.

REFERENCE

shortlist (people)   nominate someone

put (someone) forward for (something)

Awards

elect (someone)

vote for (someone)

campaign for (something / someone)

be in the running for (something)

EXPRESSIONS WITH *IN*

in mind
in no time
in particular
in spite of
in the public eye

Failure
fail spectacularly
(your) plans fall through
give up on (your) dreams

Success and failure
pursue (your) dreams

Success
fulfil an ambition
be recognised as
pull off
overcome adversity

VOCABULARY EXTRA

1 Complete the table with the nouns from the list.

> compassion | courage | dedication
> humility | persistence | resourcefulness

Noun	Adjective
1	dedicated
2	humble
3	courageous
4	resourceful
5	compassionate
6	persistent

2 Match the nouns in Exercise 1 with the definitions.

1 _____ the ability to continue doing something in a determined but sometimes unreasonable way

2 _____ a strong feeling of sympathy and sadness for the suffering of others and a wish to help them

3 _____ the quality of not being proud because you are aware of your bad qualities

4 _____ the willingness to give time and energy to something because it is important

5 _____ the ability to control your fear in a difficult or dangerous situation

6 _____ the ability to make decisions and act on your own

3 Circle the correct words.

The hero I'm celebrating is …
David Nott – a British surgeon who has shown great ¹*dedication / humility* to his job volunteering for more than 25 years with aid agencies to help people in war and disaster zones. His ²*resourcefulness / courage* is evident as he travels to dangerous places and puts his own life in danger. As he worked, his ³*persistence / resourcefulness* was evident as he saved people's lives in difficult and unusual circumstances. Thanks to his ⁴*humility / persistence*, he has not only saved people's lives, but he has also trained hundreds of doctors to carry out life-saving operations. His patients are always extremely grateful to him for his ⁵*compassion / courage* towards them. I read his book, *War Doctor*, recently and the ⁶*persistence / humility* he continues to show about the work he does is often overwhelming.

Overcoming adversity

From Pennsylvania farm girl to true heroine of American microbiology, Alice Catherine Evans (1881–1975) made one of the most medically important discoveries of the 20th century. Unable to afford college, she started her career in 1901 as an elementary school teacher. But when Cornell University offered a free class on nature to rural teachers, Alice jumped at the chance and the course of her life (and history) subsequently changed.

While taking that nature class, Alice also took a basic course in the Agricultural College, which started her interest in bacteriology. She went on to win a scholarship to Cornell, earning her a Bachelor of Science degree in Bacteriology in 1909 and then a Master of Science degree in the same field from the University of Wisconsin in 1910. Alice then got a job in the Dairy Division at the US Department of Agriculture Bureau.

Her work at the Bureau involved investigating bacteria in milk and cheese. When her appointment was made permanent in 1913, Alice became the first woman scientist to have a permanent appointment in that division of the USDA.

In 1918, through her pioneering research, she was able to show that drinking raw (unpasteurised) milk could transmit the bacterium, *bacillus abortus*, which caused brucellosis (known as Malta fever), an infectious disease passed from domestic farm animals to humans. As a result, Alice passionately advocated for the pasteurisation of milk to effectively kill this disease-causing bacterium.

However, her findings and recommendations were not taken seriously by other scientists for two reasons: 1) she was a woman; and 2) she didn't have a PhD.

But by the late 1920s, other scientists eventually came to the same conclusion as Alice, and by the 1930s, the government passed laws requiring that milk be pasteurised to prevent the disease. So while it took power in numbers to effect change, it was Alice's discovery that hastened the spread of the pasteurisation movement and, as a result, saved countless people from fever and death.

Ironically and sadly, Alice herself contracted chronic brucellosis in 1922, as a result of her research. She suffered from recurrent bouts for years because the disease never left her system.

After leaving the Department of Agriculture, Alice worked for the US Hygienic Laboratory where she made valuable contributions in the field of infectious illness, including meningitis and throat infections. In 1928, she became the first female president of the Society of American Bacteriologists (now the American Society for Microbiology). She died in 1975 at the age of 94 and was added to the National Women's Hall of Fame in 1993.

📖 READING

1 Read the article quickly and find out the significance of these dates.

1 1909 _____
2 1918 _____
3 1922 _____
4 1928 _____
5 1993 _____

2 Read the article again. Complete the profile of Alice Catherine Evans. Write a short summary of her career.

Nationality: [1]_____
Profession in early life: [2]_____
Profession in later life: [3]_____
University qualifications: [4]_____
Major discovery: [5]_____
Valuable contributions: [6]_____
Summary (maximum of 75 words):

_____
_____
_____

3 CRITICAL THINKING Read the opinions. Which ones are for (F) or against (A) women? What is your view?

1 Women are not taken seriously in science and other areas of work because they aren't as intelligent as men. ☐

2 We need to change people's views on women's abilities so they have the same rights as men. ☐

3 Women often make a big difference to the areas they work in, but they have to do it silently. ☐

4 Women can't ever be as good as men, especially the ones who choose to have children. ☐

4 Can you find another scientist who was not acknowledged at the time of their scientific research? Do some research. Write a profile of the scientist.

Writing a blog post

1 **INPUT** **Read Jamie's blog about an invention he admires. Then answer the questions.**

1 What did Mikkel Frandsen invent?   2 How does the invention work?

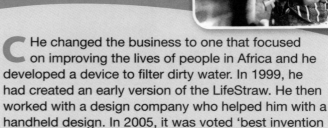

Mikkel Frandsen
– WHO IS HE?

A You've probably never heard of Mikkel Frandsen. He's an artist, a biologist and an inventor. He invented something that is 25 cm long, looks like a drinking straw but can filter up to 1,000 litres of dirty, contaminated water and keep a person hydrated for a year. It's cheap and easy to use but you probably haven't ever used one or maybe even seen a LifeStraw.

B Mikkel Frandsen was born on 1st June, 1972 in Kolding, Denmark. In 1992, at the age of 19, he went to Lagos, Nigeria on a business trip. That trip would change his life but Mikkel didn't know that at the time. He witnessed for himself first-hand the problems and consequences of not having clean drinking water – death and illness. A few years later, in 1996, he had the chance to pursue his dream when he took over his grandfather's business: manufacturing uniforms.

C He changed the business to one that focused on improving the lives of people in Africa and he developed a device to filter dirty water. In 1999, he had created an early version of the LifeStraw. He then worked with a design company who helped him with a handheld design. In 2005, it was voted 'best invention of the year' by *Time* magazine.

D In 2014, the company started a programme called Give Back. For every LifeStraw purchased, one school child in need would receive safe water for a whole year. He never imagined he would save thousands of lives, as well as produce water filters for use in homes and a LifeStraw for hikers and walkers.

E And what of the future? By 2025, half of the world's population will be living without enough clean water, but LifeStraw will have saved thousands more lives around the world and it will be continuing to help victims of natural disasters and vulnerable communities.

2 **ANALYSE** **Read and complete the sentences about Mikkel Frandsen and his invention.**

1 He didn't know that a business trip
_____ .

2 Before visiting Africa, Mikkel
_____ .

3 He had the chance to pursue his dream when _____ .

4 He never imagined he would
_____ .

3 **Match the summaries with the paragraphs.**

Paragraph A ☐
Paragraph B ☐
Paragraphs C and D ☐
Paragraph E ☐

1 explains things the inventor didn't know would happen.

2 tells us what the invention is.

3 predicts how the invention will change in the future.

4 gives us biographical information about the inventor.

4 **PLAN** **You are going to write a blog about an inventor and an invention you admire. Use the questions below to help you make notes.**

- What is the invention (e.g. the internet, a vaccine, a meat-alternative food, a new type of fabric)?
- Who played a part in inventing it? Choose one person. Are they an unsung hero or are they well known?
- Give a short biography of the inventor.
- Use your imagination. How will the invention have changed lives or had an impact on people/society in the future? What will the inventor be doing in a few years' time? What do you think?

5 **PRODUCE** **Write your blog (300–350 words). Use the questions and your notes from Exercise 4. Write your own checklist.**

✓ CHECKLIST

☐ _____
☐ _____
☐ _____
☐ _____
☐ _____

🎧 LISTENING

1 🔊 **12.02** **Listen to the dialogue and answer the questions.**

1 What is Joe really into?
2 Who is Sam fascinated by?
3 Write the name (*Sam* or *Joe*) under the photo that shows where they are going on holiday.

A _____

B _____

2 🔊 **12.02** **Listen again. Mark the sentences T (true), F (false) or DS (doesn't say).**

By the time they get back from their holidays …

1 Sam will have visited a place of historical interest. ☐
2 Sam will have eaten lots of amazing food. ☐
3 Sam will have climbed the 365 steps to the top of El Castillo. ☐
4 Joe will have climbed an inactive volcano. ☐
5 Joe will have seen wildlife you can't see anywhere else in the world. ☐
6 Joe will have fed the sea lions. ☐
7 Joe will have snorkelled with iguanas. ☐
8 both Sam and Joe will have had fantastic adventures. ☐

DIALOGUE

1 **Complete the dialogues with the phrases in the list.**

> He's dying to | I'm really looking forward to
> I'm so excited about | it can't happen soon enough
> It's going to be amazing | This time tomorrow, I'll be

1

Sarah Mum's booked a trip to Paris for the weekend.

Max Oh cool. You've been there before though, haven't you?

Sarah Yeah. It's my little brother, Oscar's birthday.
¹_____ see the Eiffel Tower.

Max Right, and what about you?

Sarah ²_____ going, too. I want to go to Montmartre.

2

Julia ³_____ in Los Angeles. Can you believe it?

Emma You've been talking about it so much. How could I forget?

Julia I can't help it. ⁴_____ finally going to Disneyland.

3

Mario Are you ready for our expedition tomorrow?

Manuel Of course. ⁵_____ .

Mario I know. I can't wait. Finally, we're going to see what's inside those caves.

Manuel I know. We've done so much training for it. All I can say is –
⁶_____ .

2 **Now write a new dialogue. Talk to a friend about a dream holiday you are going to go on. Use phrases from Exercise 1.**

PHRASES FOR FLUENCY

→ SB p.116

1 **Complete the phrases with the words in the list.**

> ages | fancy | know
> like | question | weird

1 What's not to _____ ?
2 What do you _____ doing?
3 I haven't seen you for _____ .
4 How _____ is that?
5 How should I _____ ?
6 The _____ is, … ?

2 **Put the dialogue in order.**

☐ **Cara** Of course! The 23rd of April. How weird is that?

1 **Cara** Hi, Adele. I haven't seen you for ages.

☐ **Cara** Yes, there is. There's a new James Bond film on. Do you like Bond films?

☐ **Cara** I'd like that. What do you fancy doing?

☐ **Adele** We could go to the cinema. The question is, what's on? I don't think there's anything good on this week.

☐ **Adele** I know, it's really strange, isn't it? Listen, we should go out some time.

☐ **Adele** No, we haven't seen each other since Helen's last birthday. And guess what! It's Helen's birthday today.

☐ **Adele** Of course. What's not to like? Lots of action – lots of cool gadgets!

C1 Advanced

 READING AND USE OF ENGLISH
Part 8: Multiple matching

→ SB p.118

You are going to read an article in which four people give their opinions on what it means to be a hero. For statements 1–10, choose from the people A–D. Each person may be chosen more than once.

Which person feels that

1 anyone could potentially be a hero? ☐
2 a hero is somebody who can cope with unexpected difficulties? ☐
3 ideas about what represents a hero vary widely? ☐
4 some people who are described as heroes don't really deserve it? ☐
5 a hero is somebody who challenges our emotional responses? ☐
6 a hero is somebody who can act as a role model to others? ☐
7 fictional characters make the best heroes? ☐
8 heroes have the courage to stand up for their beliefs? ☐
9 heroes are people who produce thought-provoking work? ☐
10 it's possible to make mistakes and still be a hero? ☐

WHAT IS A HERO?

WE ASKED YOU TO TELL US WHAT YOU THINK A REAL HERO IS. HERE'S WHAT YOU TOLD US.

A LILIANA: SOCIAL WORKER

Hero is a word that tends to be used very loosely these days. I think we all know what it means in relation to comic-book characters and those working in the emergency services, but it gets applied in all sorts of contexts nowadays, and not always justifiably in my view. The result is that if you ask a random sample of people, you'll get as many definitions as you have respondents. For what it's worth, the defining quality for me is strength – but not solely the physical kind. A hero is somebody whose actions are extraordinary in such a way as to inspire us. So it could be someone who doesn't think twice about running into a burning building to save lives – but it could also be someone with the strength to defend what they know to be right – even if that gets them into trouble.

B MUSTAFA: PERSONAL TRAINER

My heroes are all sports people, probably because I'm a keen athlete myself, although they come from a range of sports. They must be people I identify with in terms of their aims and approach, but they're not necessarily the champions in their particular event. Indeed, seeing how they deal with failure or with things not going to plan is what puts them in the hero category for me. I'm not looking to follow anyone's example, however, and even if they're flawed in all sorts of ways and sometimes get stuff wrong, that doesn't stop them being heroes for me. Basically, heroes aren't born – nobody has special powers or qualities – it's what you do with whatever skills and talents you have that counts, so any of us might end up in that position.

C LATA: LIBRARIAN

Heroism for me is a quality that you simply can't find in everyday life – we need to look to literature to find real heroes – but even that's a term that needs to be interpreted very broadly these days, because why shouldn't it be extended to include the classic comic-book characters and other superheroes. Personally, I admire Ironman because he uses his technical expertise to do good – he's a brilliant mechanical engineer and a very effective businessman. I'm not saying that he's perfect or that anyone should model their life on his because that wouldn't be possible. People are taken aback to hear that I regard someone like him as my hero, but he does his best to make the world a better place. What's not to like about that?

D MAGNUS: FIREFIGHTER

People sometimes describe me as a hero – but I'm just doing my job. I think a true hero is somebody creative who has the power to move us with their words or art. Think of novels you've read that have taken you to unimagined places or paintings that have made you see the world in a new way. The people who create these are heroes. They're driven by an inner force as they try to make sense of our world and pass on their discoveries to the rest of us. They have the power to make us reconsider the way we feel about things through their art. Can there be anything more heroic than that?

CONSOLIDATION

🎧 LISTENING

1 🔊 12.03 **Listen to the conversation between Owen and Tina. Who has Owen 'unfriended' on Facebook?**

2 🔊 12.03 **Listen again and choose the correct answers.**

1 What does Tina initially think about the idea of unfriending special friends on Facebook?
   A It's a great idea.
   B It doesn't make any sense.
   C It's a bit of an overreaction.

2 When it comes to communication, what are partners who are also Facebook friends at risk of doing?
   A Talking about their posts too much when they are together.
   B Falling out over things they've posted.
   C Relying too much on Facebook to share their thoughts and experiences.

3 Why might some partners fall out over posting family photos online?
   A Because one of them might think it is invading their or their family's privacy.
   B Because sometimes it feels like they've taken certain photos with Facebook in mind.
   C Because they can't agree which photos to upload.

4 Why might some people not want to know everything about their partner's life?
   A Because they like to keep an element of mystery within their relationship.
   B Because the exact details are a bit boring.
   C Because they haven't got enough time to read it all.

Ⓖ GRAMMAR

3 **Complete the sentences using three to six words including the word in brackets.**

1 Someone broke into our car last night. (got)
   Our _____ last night.
2 The workmen are installing a new kitchen for my parents. (installed)
   My parents are _____ .
3 You must report any accidents to the head office. (be)
   All _____ to the head office.
4 My exams finish on Monday morning. (afternoon)
   By Monday _____ .
5 The film I'm going to starts at 9 pm and lasts two hours. (watching)
   At 9.30 pm, I _____ a film.
6 I intended to phone you, but I forgot. (going)
   I _____ , but I forgot.

🔤 VOCABULARY

4 **Circle the correct options.**

1 I really didn't want to *lose / drop* my temper, so I just *bit / held* my tongue and said nothing.
2 I'm not going to *vote / nominate* Martha for the position because I'm thinking of putting *me / myself* forward.
3 I'm going to vote *in / for* Aya because she's campaigning *on / for* a shorter school day.
4 Luke clearly needed to *let / put* off steam and he ended up having a *go / fight* at me.
5 I didn't manage to pull it *up / off* and *failed / passed* the exam spectacularly.
6 Olivia is in the *chance / running* for the prize and she's on the *small list / shortlist*.
7 Try to stay *peaceful / calm* and not get so worked *out / up*.
8 She never gave *over / up* on her dreams and *fulfilled / completed* her ambition to become a writer.

5 **Complete the missing words.**

1 My worst trait is p_____ . I always see the worst in a situation.
2 I only asked you if I could borrow your phone. You don't need to b_____ my head off.
3 S_____ is my kind of politics – trying to make things equal for everyone.
4 His life wasn't easy and he had to o_____ a lot of adversity to get where he is today.
5 I think a_____ is something that affects young people more than they realise.
6 Their plans to open a vegetarian restaurant have all f_____ through, unfortunately.
7 Some people think c_____ is selfish because it is more about the individual than the whole of society.

DIALOGUE

6 **Put the dialogue in order.**

1	Azra	Oh no!! My mouse has stopped working.
	Azra	Very funny. Just fix it will you?
	Azra	How should I know when? I just turned the computer on and it was broken.
	Azra	It just won't respond. How weird is that? It's just died on me.
	Azra	What? Can you fix it?
	Azra	OK, but you won't be able to fix it. You're just wasting your time.
	Omer	It isn't actually broken. I know what's happened.
	Omer	I can. The question is – should I?
	Omer	Calm down. What's the problem exactly?
	Omer	Maybe I am but I can try. Now let me see. When did it stop working exactly?
	Omer	OK, this button here on the side is switched off. You just need to switch it to 'on'!
	Omer	Computer mice don't just die. Let me have a look.

 READING

7 **Read the article and answer the questions.**

1 Why are Juan's achievements remarkable?
_____

2 How did Juan get started with his hobby? _____

3 Who does Juan take to the jungle and why?
_____

4 What is the aim behind his CD?
_____

5 What was Juan's view on the link between a bird's colour and its song? How was it wrong?'
_____

6 Why does Juan think that for sighted people sound is 'invisible'?
_____

 WRITING

8 **Which of your senses do you value the most? Write a short text explaining which one and why. Think about the things that you would miss most if you lost this sense. Write about 200–220 words.**

AMAZING PEOPLE:
JUAN PABLO CULASSO

Uruguayan Juan Pablo Culasso has never known what it is to see as he was born blind. But not being able to see has not prevented him from becoming one of the top bird watchers in South America. Now, aged 35, he is a leading expert on the birds of South America, having developed an ability to locate and identify each bird by its song.

Juan's interest in nature started at an early age when his father taught him to play bird songs on the piano and took him to the natural history museum where he could handle bird specimens and feel their feathers. At the age of 12, he began to make recordings of birds and at 16 he was shown how to work a sound recorder and encouraged to go out and make recordings by his teacher Dr Santiago. It was the beginning of a lifelong passion.

Juan spends much of his time walking through the rainforests of eastern South America. He is accompanied by his guide dog Ronja who acts as his eyes and helps him navigate through the dense vegetation. Juan uses his ears to locate the bird then puts on his headphones to help him guide his microphone in the exact direction to get the best recording possible. He has made hundreds of recordings and has released a CD of Brazilian birds called *Welcome to the Atlantic Forest*, which takes the listener through an audio journey of a day in the life of the Brazilian jungle, from before sunrise to after sunset. Juan admits that he did have a problem with colours. He always imagined that the birds with the most beautiful songs were also the ones with the brightest and most beautifully coloured feathers, so he was surprised to hear that in fact the contrary was often the case and that the plainest birds had the most amazing voices.

Juan doesn't think of his blindness as a disability and instead celebrates how this has heightened his other senses. He feels that for sighted people, sound is invisible. He believes that we all have the ability to enjoy it in the way that he does but that that ability is sleeping and we're therefore not tapping into it.

PRONUNCIATION

UNIT 1
Intonation: showing emotions

1 Before you listen, read the sentences and predict how the speaker is feeling and the tone he or she might use. Write A (angry), C (cheerful), D (disappointed), E (enthusiastic), P (puzzled) or S (sympathetic) in the boxes.

   0 I told you not to tell your brother we were coming here! **[A]**

   1 Why don't we go to London this summer? Let's start making plans now! ☐

   2 I'd love to go to the party but I have to look after my little sister. ☐

   3 That's funny. I thought I had £20 in my wallet. ☐

   4 I'm sorry you're not feeling well. Would you like a cup of tea? ☐

   5 It could be worse. At least it's not raining! ☐

2 🔊 1.02 **Listen, check and repeat. Were your predictions correct?**

UNIT 2
Different ways of pronouncing c and g

1 Say the words in the list, paying attention to the sounds of the underlined letters. Write the words in the table.

accident | artificial | beneficial | biscuit
cyberspace | dangerous | decision | disagree
generally | guilty | occasionally | regular
sufficient | topic | urgently

/k/ can	
/s/ city	accident
/ʃ/ wish	
/g/ got	
/dʒ/ jump	

2 🔊 2.02 **Listen, check and repeat.**

Learn the spelling rule:
The letters *i*, *e* or *y* after *c* give the letter a soft /s/ sound. Before *i*, *e* or *y* we keep the hard /k/ sound by using the letter *k* (e.g. kite) or *qu* (e.g. antique). We can also add *u* after the *c* (e.g. biscuit).

This is the same for the letter *g* (e.g. general, giraffe and gym have the soft /dʒ/ sound; although there are exceptions, for example, get). We use the letter *u* to keep the hard /g/ sound (e.g. guilty and guitar).

UNIT 3
Unstressed words in connected speech

1 🔊 3.01 **Listen and read the sentences, putting stress marks above the stressed words in the sentences.**

   0 If I'd known how to play, I would've joined in.

   1 If I had money, I would've gone out for dinner.

   2 If she hadn't invited him, they wouldn't have met.

   3 If he hadn't missed the train, we'd be having coffee now.

   4 A kinder person would've apologised for making us wait so long.

   5 We'd still be friends if she hadn't said those things.

2 🔊 3.01 **Listen again and try to say the sentences at the same time as the speaker. You will need to use correct sentence stress to finish at the same time!**

UNIT 4
Telling jokes: pacing, pausing and punchlines

1 🔊 4.02 **Read and listen to two versions of the same joke. In one version, the speaker has not slowed down and paused at all. Which version has been told well, the first or second one?**

A man went to see the doctor and sat down to explain his problem.

'Doctor, doctor! I've got this problem,' he said. 'I keep thinking that I'm a dog. It's crazy. I don't know what to do!'

'Interesting,' said the doctor soothingly. 'Relax, come here and lie down on the sofa.'

'Oh no, Doctor,' the man said nervously, 'I'm not allowed on the furniture.'

2 🔊 4.02 **Listen again to the version of the joke that has been told well. Write S where the speaker slows down and P where they pause for effect.**

UNIT 5
Connected speech feature: elision

1 🔊 5.01 **Listen and read the sentences. Underline the pairs of words where the consonant sound at the end of the first word disappears. There are two in each sentence.**

0 The last person to leave the room must switch off the lights.

1 Millie and Frida came to the house for cake and tea.

2 Julie ran her fastest marathon last year.

3 I lost my ticket and missed the train.

4 She jumped from the building onto the cardboard boxes.

5 He travelled from France to England by boat.

2 🔊 5.01 **Listen again, check and repeat. Which two consonant sounds disappear at the ends of the words in these sentences?**

UNIT 6
Modal stress and meaning

1 🔊 6.01 **Read and listen to the sentences, paying attention to the underlined modals and verbs. Circle the one that is stressed.**

0 I might come to the football match. Who's playing?

1 Jack might like your help – even though he's very independent.

2 Are you going to Paris too? We could go together.

3 I could tell you the answer, although it wouldn't be fair on the other students.

4 Julie's lost her job; they may have to sell their house.

5 Tom may look young, but he's actually about to retire.

6 It can take two hours to get to that village by train.

2 🔊 6.01 **Listen again. This time, decide what the speaker is thinking. Tick a) or b), remembering that we stress the modal verb when we are less sure.**

0 I **might** come to the football match. Who's playing?
   a I really want to come to the match. ☐
   b I'll come to the match depending on which teams are playing. ☑

1 Jack **might** like your help – even though he's very independent.
   a The speaker thinks Jack would like your help. ☐
   b The speaker thinks Jack probably won't want your help. ☐

2 Are you going to Paris too? We **could** go together.
   a I don't really want to go with you. ☐
   b I want to go to Paris with you. ☐

3 I **could** tell you the answer, although it wouldn't be fair on the other students.
   a I might tell you the answer even if it's not fair on the others. ☐
   b I don't think I'm going to tell you the answer because it's not fair. ☐

4 Julie's lost her job; they **may** have to sell their house.
   a It's possible that they'll have to sell the house. ☐
   b The speaker thinks they will probably sell the house. ☐

5 Tom **may look** young, but he's actually about to retire.
   a Tom looks young but he isn't. ☐
   b Tom looks young to some people but not to everyone. ☐

6 It **can take** two hours to get to that village by train.
   a It often takes two hours to get to that village by train. ☐
   b If you are unlucky it will take you two hours to get to that village. ☐

UNIT 7
Connected speech feature: assimilation

1 🔊 7.01 **Listen and read, paying attention to the linking sounds. Write the words in the columns.**

> brown bird | common cold | foreign guest
> green pencil | green grass | London Bridge
> London cab | thin person

/n/ changes to /m/	/n/ changes to /ŋ/
brown bird	

2 🔊 7.01 **Listen, check and repeat.**

UNIT 8
Stress in multi-syllable words

1 **Write the words in the correct columns.**

> anticipated | comfortable | communicative
> congratulated | contribution | extremely
> fundamental | incomprehensible | materialistic
> recognised | undefeated | unrecognisable

Three syllable	Four syllable	Five syllable	Six syllable
		anticipated	

2 🔊 8.02 **Listen and check, underlining the stressed syllable in each word.**

3 🔊 8.02 **Listen again, check and repeat.**

UNIT 9
Unstressed syllables and words: the /ɪ/ phoneme

1 🔊 9.01 **Listen to the sentences and put a dot over the short /ɪ/ sound in the underlined words.**

0 The man was released when the police realised it was a case of mistak<u>e</u>n identity.

1 They <u>decided</u> they didn't have enough evidence to take the man to court.

2 Mrs Clark suffered a great miscarriage of <u>justice</u> after her children died.

3 The police <u>arrested</u> her for protesting against environmental destruction.

4 I've <u>been</u> worried about him but it turns out there's nothing wrong.

5 The letter in his <u>pocket</u> proved that he had been at the scene of the crime.

6 The police found three <u>bullets</u> at the scene of the crime.

7 They nearly sent her to prison, but <u>subsequent</u> evidence proved her innocence.

8 Many poor people around the world suffer from <u>prejudice</u>.

9 Mrs Clark was <u>convicted</u> of a crime she didn't commit.

2 🔊 9.01 **Listen again, check and repeat.**

UNIT 10
Lexical and non-lexical fillers

1 🔊 **10.01** **Listen and write the linking words in the text.**

⁰ _Hmm_ . I never even considered going to university. ¹_____, I was always going to go straight out into the world and earn some money. My dad, ²_____, disapproved of my plans. My brothers had both gone to uni and graduated, and I guess it was expected that I'd do the same. To be honest, I was, ³_____, a bit tired of learning. I just wanted to get away from all the rules and regulations and ⁴_____, see what I could do on my own. And ⁵_____, I must confess I wanted to have things like a house and a car. My friends, ⁶_____, accused me of being materialistic. I suppose they were ⁷_____ right, but I don't feel guilty about it. ⁸_____, they've all left university now with massive loans to pay off and ⁹_____, I've got a good job and a fair amount of disposable income. So no, I don't regret not going to university one bit.

2 🔊 **10.01** **Listen again and check your answers.**

3 **Lexical fillers are real words although they don't have any meaning here except to give the speaker time to think. Non-lexical fillers are words with no meaning. Write the lexical fillers in column 1 and the non-lexical fillers in column 2.**

Lexical fillers	*I mean*
Non-lexical fillers	*Er*

UNIT 11
Intonation: mean what you say

1 🔊 **11.01** **Read and listen to the same sentence said in two ways. Tick (✓) the sentence where the tone of voice is appropriate and cross (✗) where it is inappropriate.**

0 a I wish you hadn't told her – it was a secret. ✗
   b I wish you hadn't told her – it was a secret. ✓
1 a If you haven't got the time, I'll do it for you. ☐
   b If you haven't got the time, I'll do it for you. ☐
2 a You sound really stressed. Why don't you take it easy? ☐
   b You sound really stressed. Why don't you take it easy? ☐

3 a Don't worry – it's not a problem at all. ☐
   b Don't worry – it's not a problem at all. ☐
4 a Haven't you eaten yet? It's four o'clock! ☐
   b Haven't you eaten yet? It's four o'clock! ☐

2 🔊 **11.01** **Listen and repeat the sentences which are said in an appropriate way.**

UNIT 12
Shifting word stress

1 🔊 **12.01** **Listen and circle the word you hear.**

	Noun	Verb
0	**con**duct	con**duct** (circled)
1	**con**flict	con**flict**
2	**con**tract	con**tract**
3	**pre**sent	pre**sent**
4	**pro**test	pro**test**
5	**re**cord	re**cord**
6	**sus**pect	sus**pect**

2 **Write the word you circled to complete the sentences. Write N for noun or V for verb.**

0 Let's all put money in and get Jake a _present_ for his birthday. [N]
1 She was only eighteen when they asked her to _____ the orchestra. ☐
2 They have no proof, but they _____ that he stole the money. ☐
3 He broke the world _____ for the longest solar powered flight. ☐
4 The world is full of _____; we hope there will be more peace in the future. ☐
5 When you accept a job, you often need to sign a _____. ☐
6 They decided to _____ against the trees being cut down in the park. ☐

3 🔊 **12.01** **Listen, check and repeat.**

GRAMMAR REFERENCE

UNIT 1
Talking about habits

1   To talk about things that are generally (but not always) true, we can use the verb *tend to* + verb.

*My friends and I **tend to stay** home on cold evenings.*
*It **tends to rain** here in spring.*

2   We can also use the modal verb *will/won't* + infinitive. In this use, *will* does not have a future reference. This use often refers to how we expect people to behave.

*When my sister has a problem, she **will** only **tell** me about it, no one else.*
*Dad **won't let** us leave the dinner table until everyone's finished their food.*

3   When someone has a habit or does something repeatedly, and it annoys us, we can use the present continuous + *always*.

*He's **always phoning** me to ask me out, even though I've hinted that I'm not interested.*
*Our neighbours **are always making** lots of noise. They seem to have a party every weekend.*

4   We often talk about past habits using *used to* + infinitive or *would* + infinitive.

*When we lived in Japan, we **used to eat** more seafood.*
*When she was a child, she **would sit** in her room all day.*

Adverbs to express attitude

We use words like *unfortunately, admittedly, hopefully, understandably, surely, honestly* and *obviously* to show how we feel about the situation or action we're describing. They usually come at the start of the sentence.

***Unfortunately** I can't go to their party tonight.*
***Hopefully** they'll have another party, and I'll be able to go.*

UNIT 2
Past tenses with hypothetical meaning

1   With some expressions, for example, *it's time, I'd rather, I'd prefer (it if), I wish, If only* we use a past tense to talk about how we would like situations to be different.

2   We use *It's time* + past tense to say that something needs to happen soon.

*It's really late. **It's time** we went home.*

3   We use *I'd rather* + subject + past tense, or *I'd prefer it if* + past tense, to talk about how we'd prefer things to be.

***I'd rather he didn't** make that noise when he's eating.*
***I'd prefer it if** we **watched** a film rather than the football.*

4   With *It's time* and *I'd prefer* we use the infinitive when the subject of the second verb is the same as the subject of *It's time / I'd prefer*. If the subject is different, we use the past tense structure.

It's time to go. (= I/we have to go now.)
It's time you went. (= I think you have to go now.)
I'd prefer to eat curry. (= I want to eat curry.)
I'd prefer it if you cooked dinner tonight. (= I want you to cook dinner tonight; I don't want to cook.)

5   We use *I wish / If only* + past tense to talk about how we would like a present situation to be different.

***I wish** I **was** at home. (= I'm not at home.)*
***If only** I **didn't** have to go to school tomorrow.*
(= I have to go to school tomorrow.)

6   We use *I wish / If only* + past perfect tense to talk about how we regret a past situation or action.

***I wish** you **hadn't told** me that. (= You told me something I didn't want to hear/know.)*
***If only** I **had listened** to his advice. (= I didn't listen to his advice, but I now think I should have.)*

Adverbs for modifying comparatives

1   To make a contrast stronger, we can use *much* or *a lot/lots*. We can also use adverbs such as *considerably, far, significantly, notably, way* and *drastically*.

*Food is now **significantly** more expensive than last year.*
*Their new album is **way** / **far** better than the last one.*
*Her health has got **drastically** worse, I'm afraid.*

2   There are differences in register amongst these words. *Notably* and *Significantly* are used in more formal spoken contexts and in writing.

3   To make a *not as … as* construction stronger, we can use *not nearly, nothing like* and *nowhere near*.

*Your bike is **nowhere near** as good as mine.*

UNIT 3
Mixed conditionals

1   If we want to connect a hypothetical (imaginary) past with a present action or situation, then the *if* clause follows the pattern of a third conditional and the consequence clause follows the pattern of a second conditional.

*If I **had caught** the bus, I **would be** at school now.*
(= I didn't catch the bus and I'm not at school yet.)

2   If we want to connect a hypothetical (imaginary) present with a past action or situation, the *if* clause follows the pattern of a second conditional and the consequence clause follows the pattern of a third conditional.

*If his parents **earned** more money, they**'d have paid** for him to go on the school trip. (= They don't earn more money so they didn't pay for the school trip.)*

Alternatives to *if*

1   We can use other words apart from *if* when we want to talk about (real or imaginary) actions and their consequences. Some common ones are: *as long as, otherwise, provided that, suppose, imagine* and *unless*.

2   We use *as long as* and *provided (that)* to mean 'on the condition that'. We use these mainly in first conditional sentences, and usually (though not exclusively) when we are negotiating something with someone.

*You can go to the match **as long as** you tidy your room.*
*I'll tell you a secret, **provided (that)** you don't tell anyone.*

3   We use *imagine* and *suppose* in second and third conditional sentences when we are hypothesising about imaginary (present or past) situations. They are used at the beginning of sentences and are often used to introduce questions.

***Imagine** you could visit any country in the world, where would you go?*
***Suppose** you knew that one of your friends had stolen something, what would you do?*

4   *Unless* has the meaning of *if not*. It can be used in all conditional structures.

*I won't go to the dentist **unless** the pain gets worse. (= If the pain doesn't get worse, I won't go to the dentist.)*

5   We often use *otherwise* when we want to warn someone about what will happen if a condition is not met. We typically use this in first conditional sentences but we can use it in other conditionals too.

*I need to spend less money. **Otherwise** I'll have nothing left by the weekend.*

UNIT 4
Emphatic structures

1   When we want to write or say something with emphasis, we can use a cleft sentence, using *what, it* or *all*.

***It's** his facial expressions that make me laugh.*
***What** makes me laugh is his facial expressions.*
***All** I know is that he has great facial expressions.*

2   We use the word *it* when we want to focus attention on the information at the beginning of the sentence, often to correct what someone else has said or to offer an alternative opinion or idea.

It was Santos Dumont who made the first ever flight, not the Wright brothers.

3   The word *what* is used in this way to mean 'the thing that'. We use *what* in this way when we want to emphasise what comes at the end of the sentence.

***What** matters to a lot of people **is** how the government spends public money.*

4   If we want to focus on one particular thing, we can use the word *all* to mean 'the only thing that'.

***All** I want to do is go to bed.*

5   The form of these structures is as follows:
What / All + clause + *be* + clause
It + *be* + noun phrase + relative clause

Boosting

1   We use adverbs such as *certainly, undoubtedly, unquestionably* and *definitely* to make what we say sound more certain and forceful. This is known as boosting. Other common adverbs include *undeniably, clearly, absolutely, utterly, entirely, essentially, literally* and *totally*.

*She **definitely** doesn't like me.*
*That was a **totally** amazing concert.*
*Germany were **undeniably** the better team on the day.*

2   Remember the usual positioning of adverbs:
After the verb *to be*:
*It **was unquestionably** the most difficult test we'd ever done.*
Before the main verb:
*They **undoubtedly expected** to win the match.*
After auxiliaries:
*They **have clearly** not understood the instructions.*

UNIT 5
Participle clauses

In participle clauses, we use the present or past participle form of the verb, or the perfect participle, to combine two clauses that share the same subject.

1 **We use them to talk about two events that happen(ed) at the same time.**
   Taking a deep breath, he jumped into the freezing water. (= At the same time as he took a deep breath, he jumped into the water.)

2 **We use them to talk about an action that happened before the other action in the sentence.**
   Having arrived at the station, we bought our tickets. (= We arrived at the station and then bought tickets.) NB in this case we use *having* followed by the past participle.

3 **Remember, the subject of both clauses must be the same.**
   Walking down the street, a really heavy rainstorm soaked me. (This suggests the rainstorm was walking down the street.)
   Walking down the street, I got soaked by a really heavy rainstorm. (This sentence is acceptable as the subject (*I*) is the same in both clauses.)

4 **With passive structures, we use the past participle.**
   Equipped with a parachute, he jumped out of the plane.

5 **We can also use participle clauses to give reasons for something.**
   Having heard about the new museum, she decided to visit it. (= Because she heard about the new museum, she decided to visit it.)

6 **Note that participle clauses are more common in writing than in spoken language.**

Verbs of perception with infinitive or gerund

1 **Verbs of perception (e.g. see, feel, hear) can be followed by another verb either in the gerund or in the infinitive.**

2 **If we follow with a gerund, it suggests that we saw (or felt or heard) part of an ongoing action.**
   We *heard* a man *shouting* downstairs. (= A man shouted many times and we heard some of it.)

3 **If we follow with an infinitive, it suggests that we saw (or felt or heard) a complete action from beginning to end.**
   We *heard* a man *shout* downstairs. (= A man shouted and we heard this in its entirety.)

UNIT 6
Modal verbs

Modal verbs each have more than one use / meaning.

1 ***Will* and *won't* can be used to state a belief about the future.**
   I think we *will* / *won't* discover life on other planets.
   will can also be used to talk about habitual behaviour in the present.
   He *will leave* his dirty cups without washing them.
   won't can be used to express refusal.
   Their children *won't eat* vegetables, only potatoes.

2 **To hypothesise or to talk about present and future possibilities, we can use *may* / *might* / *could*.**
   Don't touch that – it *could be* dangerous.
   We *may be* home late tonight.

3 ***Can* and *may* can also be used to ask for or give permission. Here, *may* is more formal than *can* and so it is less frequent.**
   Can / *May* we *change* the channel on the TV, please?

4 ***Can* is also used to talk about general ability, and about tendencies or theoretical possibility.**
   They *can be* very rude sometimes. (tendency)
   Temperatures *can reach* up to 40 degrees in Madrid in the summer. (theoretical possibility)
   He *can lift* 100 kg above his head. (ability)

5 **As well as talking about present or future possibilities, *could* describes general past ability.**
   My grandmother *could speak* six languages.

6 ***Should* is used either to give advice, to make recommendations, or to talk about expectations.**
   I think you *should go* and lie down. (advice)
   You *should see* that film. It's great. (recommendation)
   You *should ask* before taking something. (expectation)

7 ***Must* is used to make a deduction, for strong advice, or for strong obligation.**
   You've worked hard – you *must be* tired. (deduction)
   If you go to London, you *must go* on the London Eye. (advice)
   You *must give* it back to me tomorrow. (obligation)

8 ***Mustn't* is used for prohibition.**
   We *mustn't make* a noise in here.

9 ***Can't* is used for lack of ability, or to say that something is impossible, based on deduction.**
   I *can't answer* this question. (lack of ability)
   Ninety percent of people pass that test, so it *can't be* very difficult. (deduction)

10 **We can also use *might* / *may* to express concession.**
   He *might be* rich, but I don't think he's very happy.

UNIT 7
Substitution

1 In formal situations and sometimes in written English, we can avoid repetition of nouns by using *that* (*of*) / *those* (*of*). When we are referring to people we must use *those*.

An important **question** *is* **that of** *the country's economy.*
Many **people** *like fast food, but there are* **those** *who hate it.*

2 We can avoid repeating verb phrases by using *do* / *did* / *think* / *hope* + *so*.

He says they're a great band, but I really **don't think so**.
A: *Please take these bags to my room.*
B: *I will* **do so** *immediately, Sir.*

3 To avoid repeating ideas, we can use *so* / *neither*, *nor*. The phrases take on the meaning of 'also'. The subject and object are inverted.

I didn't want to go and **neither did she**.
A: *I'm looking forward to our holiday.*
B: **So am I!**

Ellipsis

We often leave words out in English. This is known as 'ellipsis' and is especially true of informal spoken language. The words that are most frequently omitted are subject pronouns (*I* / *you*) and auxiliary verbs (e.g. *do* / *did* / *are* / *is* etc.). When the context is very clear, we often leave out verbs as well.

A *Did you have a good weekend? = Good weekend?*
B *Yes, I had a good weekend. = Yes, I did.*
A *Are you looking for someone? = Looking for someone?*
B *No, I'm not looking for anyone. = No, I'm not.*

UNIT 8
Relative clauses with determiners and prepositions

1 In relative clauses, if there is a preposition, it usually appears at the end of the clause.

He isn't someone **that** *I really want to talk* **to**.
There's a bridge **that** *you have to walk* **over**.

2 However, in formal written or spoken language, we can put the preposition before the relative pronoun. In this case the only two possible relative pronouns are *whom* (for people) and *which* (for things). In normal spoken language, we tend not to use the relative pronoun *whom* as it can sound overly formal.

There is not a single person here **to whom** *I wish to talk.*
It's a language **with which** *he had little familiarity.*

3 Sometimes the relative clause begins with a determiner e.g. *all of whom* / *some of which* / *none of whom* / *in which case*.

We invited 100 guests to the wedding, **all of whom** *came.*
One of the dishes was a very hot curry, **most of which** *was left uneaten.*
It's possible that over a hundred people will come, **in which case** *we will need more chairs.*

however / wherever / whatever, etc.

1 We can add *-ever* to *wh-* words to form the words *whatever, whoever, wherever, whenever, whichever* and *however*.

2 When we do this, the result is to create words which mean 'no matter what' (*whatever*) or 'no matter who' (*whoever*) and so on.

Whatever happens, don't panic! (= No matter what happens, don't panic.)
However hard I work, I never seem to please the boss. (= It doesn't matter how hard I work …)

3 *Whatever, wherever, whoever* and *whenever* are normally followed by a verb phrase.

Whatever **you do**, *I'll be happy.*
Wherever **he goes**, *he makes new friends.*
Whoever **is chosen** *for the job will have a great career ahead of them.*
Whenever **we have** *a party, the neighbours complain about the noise.*

4 *Whichever* is usually followed by a noun phrase. *Whatever* can also be followed by a noun phrase.

Whichever **laptop** *I buy, it has to have voice recognition.*
Whatever **day** *you want to have the party, we can arrange it.*

5 *However* is followed by an adjective or adverb.

However **cold** *the water is, we always go swimming.*
However **carefully** *he checked the numbers, he always got a different answer.*

UNIT 9
Negative inversion

1 Sometimes we bring negative or limiting adverbs and adverbial phrases to the beginning of a sentence in order to emphasise something. This is much more common in written than in spoken language but can be used in both for dramatic effect.

2 The word order of the sentence is inverted to follow the pattern of a question. When this inversion happens, we insert the auxiliary *do, does* or *did*, and we invert the auxiliary and the subject. With *be* and modal verbs, we use the auxiliary that's already there (e.g. *is / are / can / will* etc.) in the appropriate tense.

He rarely wins a match. → ***Rarely does he win*** *a match.*
We will never go back to that restaurant. → ***Never will we go*** *back to that restaurant.*

3 Some of the more common negative or limiting adverbial phrases are: *never (before) / rarely / not only … but also / under no circumstances / on no account / no sooner … than.*

Never before have I eaten *such wonderful food.*
Rarely is *a car like that seen on our streets.*
Not only did you shout *at her, you also made her cry.*
Under no circumstances are pets allowed *in here.*
On no account can you *do that.*
No sooner had we arrived than *he got up to leave.*

Spoken discourse markers

1 We use a lot of discourse markers in spoken language for a number of different purposes.

2 If we want to make it clear that we are talking about a result or outcome, we can use phrases like *as a result.*

*Her arguments were very convincing and **as a result** I changed my opinion.*

3 To show we are giving an opinion we can use a phrase like *as far as I'm concerned, to be honest, to tell you the truth* or *if you ask me.*

If you ask me*, this government is doing everything wrong.*

4 To show that we're changing the topic of a conversation, we can use a phrase like *by the way.*

*Yes, the concert was great. **By the way**, have you heard the latest CD they've released?*

5 We can show a contrast using a phrase such as *on the other hand, nevertheless* or *that said.*

*She's a great singer. **That said**, her choice of songs isn't great.*

UNIT 10
Reported verb patterns

1 There are many verbs which can be used to report what someone said – for example, *say, tell, promise, suggest, persuade, admit, recommend, apologise.* However, the patterns that follow these verbs vary.

2 Some reporting verbs are followed by (person) + preposition + gerund – for example, *accuse / blame / apologise.*

*They **apologised for** being late.*
*He **accused me of lying** about the missing money.*

3 One very common pattern is *that* + clause – this happens with verbs like *say, claim, tell, argue, emphasise,* etc.

*He **emphasised that** it was very important to read the instructions.*
*She **argued that** I did not have the right to tell her what to do.*

4 Some verbs (for example, *promise, refuse, decide*) are followed by an infinitive + *to.*

*The government **refused to reconsider** its position on the matter.*
*We **decided to take** a ten-minute break.*
*You **promised to tell** me as soon as you heard.*

However, *promise* and *decide* can also be followed by *that* + clause.

*The director **promised** [us] **that we would** be better off under her new plan.*
*They **decided that their dog** should be left outside.*

5 Some verbs (for example, *suggest, deny, regret*) are normally followed by a gerund.

*The fire officer **suggested installing** fire alarms.*
*She **regretted taking** part in the demonstration.*

6 Some verbs (for example, *invite, encourage, advise, warn*) are followed by object pronoun + (*not*) to + infinitive.

*They **invited us to join** them on their holiday.*
*I **warned him not to take** my things without asking.*

Passive report structures

1 Passive report structures occur with verbs such as *say, think, believe, know, find* and *consider.*

2 We use passive report structures to report information when the agent is unknown, understood or not important.

*Arabic **is said to be** a difficult language to learn.*

3 For reporting information about the present, the structure is subject + *be* + past participle of reporting verb + *to* + infinitive.

*She **is thought to have** a chance of becoming the next president.*

4 For reporting information (in the present) about something that happened in the past, the structure is subject + *be* + past participle of reporting verb + *to have* + past participle.

*They **are believed to have lived** on Earth tens of thousands of years ago.*

Hedging

Hedging is vague or cautious language that we use in order not to sound forceful or overly certain of something. Phrases that are often used in hedging include: *seem, appear, is believed, thought, said to*; modal verbs like *may, might, could*; and adverbs like *probably, possibly, perhaps*.

*This new version of the app **is said to** be far better.*
*The doctor said that a change of diet **might** help me.*
***Perhaps** it wasn't a good idea to do that after all.*

UNIT 11
The passive with *get*

1   We sometimes use the verb *get* instead of *be* in passive constructions, especially in informal speech and writing.

*I **got** told off by my mum and dad.*

2   We only use *get* in passive constructions with dynamic (action) verbs.

*His story **got** (was) published in a newspaper, but it wasn't believed by many people.*

3   We usually use the *get* passive when there is a clear good or bad effect.

*She **got** injured in a car accident.*
*I **got** offered a new job in the department.*

4   Sometimes *get* is used rather than *be* to distinguish active from stative meaning of a verb and therefore make it clear that an action is involved.

*The car **was** damaged.* (= state or action)
*The car **got** damaged.* (= action)

5   *Get* is also used in passive constructions when something happens unexpectedly or accidentally.

*The bus hit a lorry and a lot of people **got** hurt.*

Causative *have*

1   This structure is formed with the verb *to have* + object + the past participle of the main verb.

2   It is used to make it clear that another person performs an action for us because we asked them to, or paid them to.

*I **had** my living room **painted**.* (= I paid a painter to paint it)

3   It is also used when a person (often an unknown person) does something unwanted and/or unpleasant to us.

*The company **had** its computers **hacked**.* (= the company did not want or ask for this to happen)

4   It is also possible, in informal language, to use the verb *get* instead of *have* – the meanings are the same.

*I **got** my mobile phone **repaired**.*

Modal passives

1   To form a present passive using a modal verb, we use modal verb + *be* + past participle.

*These animals **can be found** in several countries in Europe.*

2   To form a past passive using a modal verb, we use modal verb + *have been* + past participle.

*The wall paintings **might have been painted** more than a hundred thousand years ago.*

UNIT 12
Future perfect; future continuous

1   We use the future continuous tense to refer to an action that will be in progress at or around a specific time in the future. It is formed with *will* + *be* + gerund.

*This time tomorrow we'**ll be flying** to Lisbon.*
*Don't phone me next Friday morning – I'**ll be taking** an exam.*

2   We use the future perfect tense when we have a certain moment in the future in mind as we describe / reference an action that happened before that moment. It is formed with *will* + *have* + past participle.

*At 8 o'clock tomorrow night, our plane **will have arrived** in Lisbon.*
*By midday next Friday, my exam **will have finished**.*

Future in the past

1   When we want to talk about the future as seen from the past, we can use *was/were going to* or *would*.

*Last year, I **was going to have** a party for my birthday but in the end, I didn't.*
*I decided not to have a party because I wasn't sure that people **would come**.*

2   We tend to use *would* or *wouldn't* when we are referring to a future possibility or an idea.

*I decided not to take the driving test because I thought I **would fail**.*

3   We tend to use *was/were going to* when we are referring to a definite plan for the future.

*The government **was going to increase** the tax, but people complained too much.*

4   There is more certainty that the future plan or event will take place with *was/were going to* than with *would*.

IRREGULAR VERBS

Base form	Past simple	Past participle
be	was / were	been
bear	bore	borne
beat	beat	beaten
become	became	become
begin	began	begun
bend	bent	bent
bet	bet	bet
bite	bit	bitten
blow	blew	blown
break	broke	broken
breed	bred	bred
bring	brought	brought
broadcast	broadcast	broadcast
build	built	built
burn	burned / burnt	burned / burnt
buy	bought	bought
can	could	–
catch	caught	caught
choose	chose	chosen
come	came	come
cost	cost	cost
cut	cut	cut
deal	dealt	dealt
dive	dived / dove	dived
do	did	done
draw	drew	drawn
dream	dreamed / dreamt	dreamed / dreamt
drink	drank	drunk
drive	drove	driven
eat	ate	eaten
fall	fell	fallen
feed	fed	fed
feel	felt	felt
fight	fought	fought
find	found	found
flee	fled	fled
fly	flew	flown
forbid	forbade	forbidden
forget	forgot	forgotten
forgive	forgave	forgiven
freeze	froze	frozen
get	got	got
give	gave	given
go	went	gone
grow	grew	grown
hang	hung	hung
have	had	had
hear	heard	heard
hide	hid	hidden
hit	hit	hit
hold	held	held
hurt	hurt	hurt
keep	kept	kept
know	knew	known
lay	laid	laid
lead	led	led
leap	leaped / leapt	leaped / leapt
learn	learned / learnt	learned / learnt

Base form	Past simple	Past participle
leave	left	left
lend	lent	lent
let	let	let
lie	lay / laid	lain
light	lit	lit
lose	lost	lost
make	made	made
mean	meant	meant
meet	met	met
overcome	overcame	overcome
pay	paid	paid
put	put	put
quit	quit	quit
read /riːd/	read /red/	read /red/
ride	rode	ridden
ring	rang	rung
rise	rose	risen
run	ran	run
say	said	said
see	saw	seen
seek	sought	sought
sell	sold	sold
send	sent	sent
set	set	set
shake	shook	shaken
shine	shone	shone
shoot	shot	shot
show	showed	shown
shut	shut	shut
sing	sang	sung
sink	sank	sunk
sit	sat	sat
sleep	slept	slept
speak	spoke	spoken
speed	sped	sped
spend	spent	spent
spill	spilled / spilt	spilled / spilt
split	split	split
spread	spread	spread
stand	stood	stood
steal	stole	stolen
stick	stuck	stuck
strike	struck	struck
swear	swore	sworn
sweep	swept	swept
swim	swam	swum
swing	swung	swung
take	took	taken
teach	taught	taught
tear	tore	torn
tell	told	told
think	thought	thought
throw	threw	thrown
understand	understood	understood
wake	woke	woken
wear	wore	worn
win	won	won
write	wrote	written